MW01028695

THE
SEALED BOOK
OF MORMON

Translated from the Plates of Mormon
By the Gift and Power of God

Published by
United Literary Order of the Last Days, LLC
Joseph Fredrick Smith, President

Contents

FOREWORD

The value of words written in a book is determined somewhat by those who read them. Of the many books that I have read from time to time, I find value in some and no value in others. When the Book of Mormon came forth in the 1830s it was met with much criticism and cast aside even by those who were most eager to be engaged in the work of the Lord. Yet there were many who were very interested, mainly those who had come from Europe and had a foundation in the works of the Protestant Movement—those who had found a weakness in their doctrine that did not match with the Scriptures they had. To these students, the words of the Book of Mormon held much value and shed the momentum of light necessary in the Lord's quest for a people of perfection.

When Joseph Smith Jr translated the Book of Mormon from the golden plates, there was a portion that remained sealed. This portion was not to be opened until the Lord desired that work to come forth. That day has arrived. The words delivered in this translation will be considered to be of great value for those who study them with a pure heart—and who will step into the work of God's hand as He prepares a people in righteousness, worthy to be found in the Holy City, the New Jerusalem, in the land of Zion.

This sacred book will also be met with much criticism as was the Book of Mormon in my great-grandfather's time. Many have spoken out against this work, but they are unable to show any positive evidence to prove their claims. But I can testify of the truth of these things. I held those golden plates in my hands, and while they were in my hands I was engulfed in the Holy Spirit to the point of being almost completely overcome. Man cannot fake the presence of the Holy Spirit.

I was able to turn the very same plates that my great-grandfather had turned. I could recognize some of the very symbols that he had written for Martin Harris to deliver to the learned man. I was present when the top 42 plates of the sealed part were released in preparation for translation. Now this translation is available to the believers of the Book of Mormon!

It is a joy that I can be a part of the work of God that began in the hands of Joseph Smith Jr. It is a joy to see the hope of the city, New Jerusalem—the City of Zion—and to see that work roll on until all that God has purposed will be accomplished; this work of God includes the invitation to the descendants of Lehi and all the children of Israel. May God pour out His blessings as we join together for the cause of Zion.

Joseph Fredrick Smith

PREFACE

Given the nature and origin of this book, just as it was with the Book of Mormon, translated by the power and gift of God, but in two different languages, a brief explanation of the translator is needed in this preface, as described below.

It is very complex to try to explain how two transparent stones allowed me to see words, both in Portuguese which is my native language, as well as in English, a language unknown to me and with little understanding of the placement of words. But for the eight witnesses of the plates that came from the USA and the other three who are from Brazil, it is possible to have a vague idea of how this worked in my mind.

In order for the witnesses to have this vague perception of how the stones worked, I was allowed to shine a ray of light through the stones and get an image on the wall to show the witnesses the icons that were filled in my mind with the necessary information. However, although the stones showed me the words described in the characters, it was a great responsibility to translate this unknown language, whose words mostly do not exist anymore in the current dialect of humanity. Thus, I had to choose between the many words that the stones presented in these pictures that appeared in my mind, those that are current and understandable in our modern day, with the purpose of stating the text and its context in a reliable form, without there being any flaws in the understanding of that which Mormon and his son Moroni truly wrote for our understanding.

I now fully understand why some anachronisms exist in the Book of Mormon, like the word "steel," which is so commonly used by the critics of Joseph Smith Jr; since this word could not exist in the records of a people who lived before the word pronounced "steel" properly be created among men. Certainly, among the many words that appeared through of the interpreting stones for Joseph to choose, with the purpose to describe the bow of Nephi, while translating the Book of Mormon, "steel" was selected by Joseph to portray then, a word non-existent in the nineteenth century, with the purpose of describing reliably the metal alloy described in the original Nephite record, but which, would be a dead word for the readers' understanding from the Book of Mormon, both in the first years of the restoration as well as for the future generations. This differs from a personal name for example, Mormon, whose pronunciation has long ceased to exist in the Americas, but which can be understood in reading the Book of Mormon as portraying a character in contrast to the description of an bow, whose original pronouncement never would be understood by readers of the Book of Mormon as a metal alloy, since, generally, the bows of antiquity are portrayed in history as being of wood and not of iron.

Another phenomenon caused by the reading of the plates through of the Nephite interpreters, occurred every time the record quoted texts of the scriptures, referring me to the context of the bibles, whether they were parts of the New World Translation or the João Ferreira de Almeida, version in Portuguese, the Book of Mormon LDS and any other scripture I had read before, making me write what already existed in my memory, but with slight changes in some passages. Certainly this was also the case with Joseph Smith Jr. that led him to rewrite part of the King James Bible in the passages of the Book of Mormon where he recites part of the scriptures, for certainly it should have been the only Bible he read before the translation of the Book of Mormon.

Since this book does not reveal a new doctrine, but only a knowledge that was hidden from human understanding until now, the translator of this work recommends to the reader, whose desire is to obtain a confirmation of its divine nature, in being an avid researcher, diligently following the references below each verse and reflecting carefully in their general context. It is therefore imperative to look a little beyond our traditions and finally to ask God in the name of Jesus Christ if these things are not true and, by the power of the Holy Spirit, God will show you the truth.

In relation to the current rumors that the Lord retained part of the translation because of the hardness of heart of His people in these last days, of the forty-two plates that were released with the opening of the first seals, only nineteen are translated in this book. As for the amount of content of the other plates of this sealed set, it is important to emphasize that it will be unveiled only when the people of the church are living in accordance with these first teachings revealed here.

In addition, early on when the plates were announced by Brother Joseph Fredrick Smith and Brother Bob Moore, many were surprised by the translator's claim that the sealed portion would be divided in two parts. It seemed to contradict all that the Latter-day Saints had already understood on this issue, and many ridiculed their claims. The scriptures cite at least two passages that mention the sealed portion of the plates of the Book of Mormon, which together, claim that the sealed portion will be opened in two periods of time different from one another.

1 - The first refers to a rebellious and obstinate people who honor the Lord with their lips, but who turned their hearts away from Him because of the precepts of men. [RLDS 2Nephi 11:143-147 / LDS 2Nephi 27:21-26]

1a - And that these rebellious and obstinate people will be the people of Zion in the last days, for how much they boast that all is well in

Zion and deny these new scriptures. [RLDS 2Nephi 12:31-39 / LDS 2Nephi 28:25-31]

1b - Also, it refers to the man who is to read the sealed part as the one who will deliver his words to a rebellious and obstinate people. [RLDS 2Nephi 11:146 / LDS 2Nephi 27:24-25]

1c - And, it is to this rebellious and obstinate people that God intends to remind you "for the second time" of the covenants he made with his people in the opening of the fullness of times in the early days of the restoration. [RLDS 2Nephi 12:42 / LDS 2Nephi 29:1]

1d - After translating the part that concerns you, the translator of the sealed portion "will seal the plates again unto the Lord." [RLDS 2Nephi 12:79-80 / LDS 2Nephi 30:3]

2 - The second part, on the other hand, refers to a future time when the people of the covenant are pure in heart and exercise the same faith as the brother of Jared. [RLDS Ether 1:98-100 / LDS Ether 4:5-6]

2b - The second part also refers to Jesus Christ himself as the one who is to reveal the things that the brother of Jared saw, to a pure people in the final part of the fullness of times [RLDS Ether 1: 101 / LDS Ether 4:7]

The Sealed Book of Mormon, therefore, appears in these last days according to the revealed prophecies, both in the Bible and in the Book of Mormon.

For more information contact our website -
https://www.forthecauseofzion-usa-brazil.org

THE TESTIMONY OF THREE WITNESSES

By the power and mercy of our Heavenly Father and our Master and Redeemer, yes, Jesus Christ, we bear our witness to all nations.

The nature of this testimony is to briefly describe what we have seen, heard and touched:

After some time with Mauricio Berger, who told us about the events on Mount Agudo, we decided to accompany him to the mountain. We can say that everything we have seen there has an extraordinarily sacred character. The prayers and praises offered to the Lord in that place, seeking to do the will of the Father, resulted in the visit of celestial beings; the instructions received directly from the Angel Moroni, are events that have marked our lives forever and ever. We squeezed his hand and received from him the Golden Plates, the translating stones and the Sword of Laban, formerly in possession of the Prophet Joseph Smith Jr. This sublime circumstance had a powerful effect on our beliefs by enlarging our perception of this great and marvelous work.

We affirm that, by the power of God, the Sealed Book of Mormon will be translated, contained in the plates.

We know, therefore, that the translation will take place in two time periods. The first part that belongs to Maurício Berger (in fulfillment of the prophecy of 2 Nephi 27: 21-26 LDS, or even 2 Nephi 11: 143-147 RLDS), with the intention of calling His people again to repentance. Upon completion of the translation, we understand that will be fulfilled what is written in 2 Nephi 30: 3 LDS, or 2 Nephi 12:80 RLDS – where it is clear this Record will be sealed back to the Lord in accordance with Ether 4: 7 LDS or Ether 1: 101 RLDS. Qualifying your people to receive the second part.

We place our witness at the disposal of the world, with a deep sense of gratitude and a total sense of responsibility towards God who directs this work. We solemnly affirm that by our fidelity to this testimony our garments will be clean at the last day.

In vain will be the one who stands up against the work of God. Honor and glory be for ever and ever, the Father, his son Jesus Christ and the Holy Spirit, in whom we entrust the conclusion of this glorious work. Amen.

Joni Batista, Valdeci Machado, and Wagner Zeppenfeld

THE TESTIMONIES OF EIGHT WITNESSES

We declare in the name of Jesus Christ that on Sunday, March 4, 2018, Maurício Artur Berger, the translator of the first part of the sealed plates, showed to us the golden plates which are covered on both sides with fine engravings; that we held the plates and turned the pages; and we closely examined the plates, which have the appearance of gold, and are bound together by three rings, which are silver in appearance; and we examined the characters thereon, which are exceeding fine and intricately engraved. By our examination and the confirmation of the Holy Spirit we have the assurance that they are the plates of Mormon. And we give our names unto the world, to witness unto the world that which we did both behold and handle before each other, as God bears this our witness. We beheld and handled the interpreters, by which these engravings will be translated by the gift and power of God.

We further declare that in our presence the seals were removed which had tightly bound the greater portion of the plates. We beheld and examined the plates that were newly loosed, which have an exceeding luster with indented engravings.

Further, we bear record that the more part of all the plates remain sealed and are to come forth by the will of Jesus Christ in his own due time, and that we beheld and marveled to see the exquisite cover of the sealed book, that depicts upon the entire plate a carefully crafted and intricate image of the promised return of the heavenly city Zion, and that these things are to remain sealed until they are revealed by Christ to his people when they are prepared and found worthy.

We admonish all nations, kindreds, tongues and people to repent and come unto Christ and heed the words which he gives, that your souls may be found spotless at the last day.

Joseph F. Smith, Samuel S. Gould, Gary Metzger, Tyler Crowell, Kelvin Henson

In addition, in June 2018 another viewed and held these plates and is willing to give his name to the world to testify that the translator did in fact have these plates from which this record has come.

Amos Johnson

Because two of the original witnesses abdicated their right and opportunity to be promoters of this work, two substitutes were permitted in December 2018 to view the plates and are willing to testify and give their names to the world.

Melva Cackler, Roberta Chinnery

14

WORDS OF MORONI

1 And now behold, I desire to speak unto those who shall have the words of this book in their hands, after the Lord has stretched forth His arm upon the Gentiles in the latter days[1]. For, behold there shall be many of the <u>Gentiles, and also of the Jews</u>, that shall not harden their hearts concerning the words of this book which Nephi prophesied, when this book shall be revealed unto the children of men, and written unto the Gentiles and sealed again to the Lord[2]. [1]

RLDS - 2Nephi 12:40-41 / LDS - 2Nephi 28:32 | [2] RLDS - 2Nephi 12:79-80 / LDS 2 Nephi 30:3

2 But, behold, many shall believe the words of this book, and rejoice to know that it proceedeth out of the hand of God, and from their eyes will fall the scales of the darkness that prevents them from seeing in their fullness the truth sent from the heavens to the children of men, and before many generations pass, they will begin to coalesce in true knowledge, and they will become a pure and pleasing people in the sight of the Lord upon all the inhabited earth.

3 And it shall come to pass that the Lord God will again begin His work among all nations, tribes, tongues, and peoples, to effect in these times, already appointed by the Lord, the full Restoration of all things, of which God spake by His servants, the prophets[1]. [1] RLDS

2Nephi 12:83-86 / LDS 2 Nephi 30:6-7; Acts 3:19-21

4 Therefore it is in these days that the Lord invites His people: Come to Me O ye Gentiles, and I will show you things greater than these. Yea, the knowledge that is hidden because of the hardness of their hearts. Come to Me O ye house of Israel, and great things shall be revealed to you that the Father has reserved for you from the foundation of the world and have not come to you because of your unbelief.

5 Behold, the time has come for you to tear this veil that leads you to remain in this terrible state of iniquity and hardness of heart and blindness of mind, for the words that come from this record, *The*

Sealed Book of Mormon, are like the hard tip of the mallet that shatters the hardness of the rock that covers your hearts hardened by your traditions and as the fire of the refiner who refines and purifies the filth of his thoughts stained by the precepts of men[1]. [1] RLDS Ether 1:109-112 / LDS Ether 4:13-15; Jeremiah 23:29

6 In those days the Lord will stretch out His hand a second time in order to reclaim His people, who are of the house of Israel, and to do a marvelous work among them for the purpose of remembering the covenants which He made with the sons of men, and to fulfill the promises made to Nephi concerning the descendants of Lehi, his father, in order to recover the remnants of his seed and so that the words of this book, written by the seed of Nephi, come to the seed of his father in the last days and to the knowledge of the house of Israel[1]. [1] RLDS 2Nephi 12:42-44 / LDS 2Nephi 29:1-2

7 Behold, I am Moroni the son of Mormon, and my father was a descendant of Nephi, who was the son of Lehi our patriarch, who was the son of Shaphan, coming from a family of scribes of the kingdom of Judah, and of the tribe of Joseph, by the seed of Manasseh[1], just as one reads in the genealogy of Lehi by his own record described in the first part of these plaques that my father Mormon compiled. [1] RLDS Alma 8:3 / LDS Alma 10:3

8 Shaphan was the scribe secretary of king Josiah in the days when Hilkiah the high priest found under the altar of the temple in Jerusalem the ancient records of Moses[1], and among them the book of the law and the sealed book itself of the things that Moses saw when he was snatched to Heavenly Zion[2]. [1] 2 Kings 22:8 | [2] Hebrews 12:20-23; RLDS 1 Nephi 6:3; D&C 22:1, 22:24a-25 / LDS 1 Nephi 19:23; Moses 1:1, 40-42

9 And it came to pass in the first days of the reign of Zedekiah, for how much Lehi returned from Babylon together with Gemariah, the son of Hilkiah, when they were jointly commissioned by the king of Judah to go to Nebuchadnezzar, king of Babylon, and they took with them a letter from Jeremiah the prophet destined for the elders, the

priests and the prophets, and all the people exiled in the land of Shinar, that the LORD appeared to him in a pillar of fire and after that event he was no longer called by the birth name Elasah. But he became known by the name that God called him, Lehi, which corresponds to an abbreviation of Eliasib, whose meaning is, "by means of whom God restores[1]". [1] Jeremiah 29:1-3

10 Behold, I, Moroni, am the same as I told you before, that if possible I would make known all things, but I was instructed to seal my father's records and with it the record that the Lord asked me to write about what the brother of Jared saw, because the things he has seen are beyond the understanding of the Gentiles until they repent of their iniquity, and become pure before the Lord, and begin to exercise faith in the Son of God as did the brother of Jared.

11 Nevertheless I was commanded by the Lord to separate into three sets the whole record contained in the plates of Mormon in order to be revealed in three periods of times.

12 The first set is a preparatory appendix of the second, and the second of the third. The first serves to constitute an alliance between God and the Gentiles through repentance, and constitutes an open record, to be given in preparation for the people to understand the greater things when they will be revealed.

13 And if they do not harden their hearts when the second part comes, they will not only know the mysteries of God through the first part, but will receive more, a little here, another little there, line upon line; precept upon precept, until they know the mysteries of God through the revelation of the second part, to the understanding of all things concerning His church in the last days[1]. [1] RLDS Alma 9:15-18 / LDS Alma 12:9-10

14 But the reverse will come to those who possess the first part of the records compiled by my father, Mormon, in the last days, yea in the days of the Gentiles, but who will not be willing to meditate upon it in their hearts, so little will avail themselves of the gift superimposed on a promise transcribed by me, Moroni, and which corresponds to the first two parts of my father's writings, since I have registered "these my words as an exhortation," before even sealing 'these records,' corresponding to more than one sealed record, because at no time did I say 'this record' when I mentioned that I would be sealing 'these records[1].' [1] Moroni 10:2 - RLDS and LDS

15 "And I exhort you again, if God deems it prudent for you to read these records, if you have only the desire to understand the truth about them and from your heart meditate on their words, then I exhort you to ask God, the Eternal Father, in the name of Christ, if these things are not true; and if you ask with a sincere heart and with a true intention to know, having faith in Christ, then He will manifest to you the truth of them by the power of the Holy Spirit, for through the Holy Spirit you may know the truth of all things[1]." [1] RLDS Moroni 10:4-5 / LDS Moroni 10:4

16 And it shall come to pass with those who harden their hearts to this second part, when it shall be revealed unto the children of men, that even the knowledge of the first part will be taken away from them and they will remain attached to the precepts of men[1]; they will honor the Lord with their lips but they will be far from His ways[2]; they will be convinced of their faith in the first part previously revealed of these records saying, we have enough, and we are not ready for more scriptures. From this will be taken even what little of the knowledge they have until they have nothing left but their traditions[3]. [1] RLDS Alma 9:17-21 / LDS Alma 12:10-11 | [2] RLDS 2Nephi 11:143-146 / LDS 2Nephi 27:21-25 | [3] RLDS 2 Nephi 12:30-38 / LDS 2Nephi 28:24-30

17 In turn, this set corresponding to the second part which I, Moroni, foretold in a double prophecy revealed to me from Jesus Christ, whose context exposes both the emergence of this *book sealed of Mormon* that must be revealed before the coming of our Lord in the sight of His disciples in the last days, as well as the record of the seven seals that my father, Mormon, foresaw in this record, that our

Lord alone is worthy to open the rest of the seals which he contains in the sealed set of these plates of Mormon, through the events which were foretold upon the nations of the earth[1] after their coming upon Zion in the New Jerusalem and the seven events which will henceforth unfold with the children of men, all foretold in these records, which by it Jesus Christ will be revealed to those who will have the faith of the brother of Jared[2], before the coming of Heavenly Zion and the Tent of God be established forever among the sons of man and the Kingdom of our Lord subdue all nations under His terms. [1] **RLDS D&C 98:5a** / LDS D&C 101:23; D&C 77:6; **Revelation 5:5** | [2] **RLDS Ether 1:101** / LDS Ether 4:7

18 For it was revealed to me in this mixed vision that I obtained from these final events, that before the Lord came to unveil the fullness of His mysteries, that the revelations which the Lord had made to be written by His servant John, should be manifested in the eyes of all the people before His coming. And that these revelations, transcribed by my father, Mormon, in these sealed records, should serve as a reminder to the covenant children that the work of the Father truly began over all the inhabited land. It is at this time that the Lord calls His people to repentance a second time and invites them to come to Him in order to believe in His gospel[1]. [1] **RLDS 2 Nephi 12:42** / LDS 2 Nephi 29:1

19 It is at this time that the word that the Lord revealed to me, Moroni, is fulfilled, when He said: "Behold, when you tear this veil of unbelief that leads you to remain in your terrible state of iniquity and hardness of heart and blindness of mind, the great and marvelous things which were concealed from you before the foundation of the world will be revealed to you - yea when the revelations which I have made to be written by My servant John were manifested before the eyes of My people before My coming, then shall ye know that the great and the wonderful work of the Father truly began on the whole face of the Earth[1], so that all men may for the last time repent, even to the ends of the earth if they so desire, and come to Me, Jesus Christ, and believe My gospel, before I come to My temple[2] and delineate the boundaries of My kingdom, where there will be those who are loyal to Me, and no one will be allowed to cross their borders." [1] **RLDS Ether 1:111-114** / LDS Ether 4:15 -17 | [2] **RLDS D&C 38:5b; D&C 42:10c; D&C 65: 1d** / LDS D&C 38:22; D&C 42:35-36; D&C 65:5

20 On this day alone in Zion there will be protection, and in the New Jerusalem a refuge for the fellow citizens of the saints. Also in those days when the things I selected are revealed, about which I wrote that they should not be touched until such time as God judged it prudent to reveal these things in the future, then in that moment when they are brought to light by the one who is to read the words contained therein, it will occur just as in the previous days of times, that this other man of whom I have written, that he will have the privilege of showing these plates to those who will help bring this work to light. Initially they will be shown to three by the power of God, who will know with certainty that these things are true. And through the mouths of these three witnesses these things will be firmly established[1]. And no one else will see, except a few, according to the Holy Spirit, and they shall testify together with the power of God, also by His word, first uttered by the mouth of the ancient prophets, of whom the Father, and the Son, and the Holy Spirit will testify against the fallen and ruined world in the last days[2].

[1] **RLDS Ether 2:1-3** / LDS Ether 5:1-4 | [2] **RLDS Ether 2:3** / LDS Ether 5:4

21 As for me, Moroni, the Lord made me see when I was projecting the seals for these plates, which should contain two cylindrical metal pieces that would transpose all sealed set of plates. But with two internal heads to contain the remainder of the plates, where there will be another six heads of seal, according to the circumstances that Christ will reveal them in the times designated by Him, after His coming at the temple in Zion. Behold, this, come after this book of which I have spoken, which shall first be revealed to the Gentiles, that they may repent of their abominations and sins, and so shall there be still other records in this set of plates which shall remain united by these two inner heads, and must be sealed again by the one who will write the record of this first part, because not everything will be revealed in his days with the opening of the first seals, in order to preserve its content[1] so that he will reveal the rest of the plates when the Lord finds it prudent in the future, when in the end, the children of the covenant, which will come after the translation of this first set to regroup in a single fold under the name given to His chosen ones, for which your church should be known in the last days[2]. [1] RLDS 2Nephi 12:79-80 / LDS 2Nephi 30:3 | [2] RLDS 3Nephi 12:16-18 / LDS 3Nephi 27:3-8

22 Then the Lord shall descend from the heavens with sounds of trumpets accompanied by a chariot entourage, and horses and wheels of fire, which shall cover the heavens as the clouds cover the earth and all the nations that have pierced Him shall feel ashamed, and the people of the world of mankind, being afraid, shall flee without direction from their dwellings, and as reptiles, shall hide themselves in their slits[1], and a storm will sweep the four corners of the earth as if by a strong wind that would fill the four corners of the sky, when finally the Lord comes down in His temple, not to bring peace among the nations, but to annihilate those who ruin the earth[2], yea, to set fire to the chaff, bound in bundles, which are churches in the field of the world, for His wheat shall be sheltered in His vineyard, in the harness of the Lord, in Zion. [1] RLDS D&C 98:5a, 5g / LDS D&C 101: 23, 32; Micah 7: 15-17 | [2] Revelation 11: 18

23 After these days of great uproar among the nations of the earth, the Lord will come to His Temple[1] and redeem His church to make it a holy property and give it an eternal name — rescuing what was formerly lost, Church of Christ, and establishing His people perpetually upon His everlasting gospel[2]. [1] RLDS D&C 1:6c; D&C 42: 8b, 10c; D&C 108:1a / LDS D&C 1:36; D&C 42:36; D&C 133:2 | [2] Psalms 24: 8-10 IV.

24 I Moroni, I gave continuity in writing and compiling the records given to me by my father Mormon[1]. It was then, when my father was sixty-five years old, that he found himself tired[2] to pursue his record, for how much his hands have lost the vitality and the fingers the sensitivity to carve the characters in the metal sheets, and at night, under the light of the lamp, his eyes weakened with the reflection of the plates. It was then that my father, Mormon, decided to hide the records on Mount Cumorah after taking them out of the library of Shim, all records previously compiled by him from this place, except for these few plates that contain a summary made by my father, and the other twenty-four plates found by the people of Limhi in the days of Mosiah in regard to the Jaredite record, and that I have been entrusted to complete their work, for inasmuch as the other records assigned to him by the hand of the Lord[3], beginning with the plates of Nephi, along with the books that my father examined[4], and which constitute the records of the prophets, from Jacob to King Benjamin, among which my father had chosen to finish his resume, together with the records which were sealed by the ancient prophets and preserved by the hand of the Lord for a wise, future purpose. [1]

RLDS Words of Mormon 1:2-3 / LDS Words of Mormon 2 | [2] **RLDS Mormon 3:7-8** / LDS Mormon 6:6 | [3] **RLDS Mormon 3:7-8; 1:3-4; 2:25** /LDS Mormon 6:6; 1:3; 4:23 | [4] **RLDS Words of Mormon 1:4-7** / LDS Words of Mormon 3, 4

25 Among the account made by my Father of the plates of Nephi, among them is the record of Lehi, the patriarch who came from Jerusalem; the records of Nephi, the son of Lehi; the record of Jacob, the son of Lehi; the record of Enos, son of Jacob; the record of Jarom, the son of Enos; and the record of Omni, the son of Jarom.

26 From the plates which were selected by my father in which the prophecies concerning the coming of Christ have been fulfilled even to our day, beginning with a brief introduction transcribed as 'The Words of Mormon,' is found condensed in summary the record of Mosiah; the record of Alma; the record of Helaman and other

22

records with the name of Nephi, and three other records which were employed by my father and me as the Book of Mormon; the book of Ether, which contains a record of the Jaredites, extracted by me, Moroni, from the twenty-four plates of the people of Limhi, except the part of the vision of the brother of Jared, which I have transcribed from the rest of the twenty-four plates, but which will not be revealed until the Lord comes to His temple to purify the sons of Levi[1], and the book I wrote soon after, which bears my name, as the Book of Moroni. [1] Malachi 3:1-3; RLDS D&C 1:6c; D&C 108:1a / LDS D&C 1:36; D&C 133:2

27 From the sealed records of the prophets, which were summarized and compiled on this set of plates by my father, Mormon, among them is *The Sealed Book of Moses*[1], written by the hand of Moses himself in scrolls of hides, and which had been sealed by his signet ring, and which was later compiled on the plates of the people of Nephi which contains the records of the prophets, containing the things he saw concerning this world and the prophecies concerning the judgments of God that would fall on the inhabited earth, each in their respective dispensations, for how much King Josiah himself did not endure these prophecies, whose record was found together with the book of the law, when Hilkiah, the high priest in Jerusalem undertook the restoration of the temple, coming to consult Huldah[2], the prophetess, to know if any of these terrible events described in this sealed book of Moses would have to fall upon the chosen nation of his days. [1] RLDS 1Nephi 6:3; D&C 22:24a-25 / LDS 1Nephi 19:23; Moses 1:40-42; 2 Kings 22:8-20 | [2] 2 Kings 22:14

28 But of all records of Moses, my father Mormon compiled only a summary, leaving aside the prophecies and pointing to a wise, future purpose, the issues related to the Melchizedek priesthood among the covenant people from the beginning to the end of all preconceived times, for how much the remaining content of this book of Moses

will be on the plates that will be revealed only when Christ comes to His temple in the last days.

29 Therefore, it was in the care of the family of Lehi, whose name was Elasah[1], before the Lord called him, for inasmuch as his father Shaphan, as well as his forefathers before him, was the secretary and scribe of the king of Judah, and with that he was acquainted with the language of his ancestors and also of the Phoenicians, as well as of the Chaldeans, from which Abraham proceeded, and also of the Egyptian writing[2], for how much the Hebrews were taken captive by Pharaoh after Joseph perished in Egypt, until Moses delivered them.

[1] **Jeremiah 29:1-3** | [2] **2 Kings 22:3; RLDS 1Nephi 1:1 / LDS** 1Nephi 1:2

30 Thus, Lehi had been commissioned by the Lord to protect this record of Moses, and directed to cross the great waters soon after returning from Babylon, when in the early days of the reign of Mattaniah, which had been given the name of Zedekiah, he was sent with Gemariah, son of Hilkiah, to Nebuchadnezzar with a message from the king of Judah. It was at this time that Jeremiah the prophet sent to the care of Elasah, that is, by Lehi, a letter to the chief elders of Judah and Jerusalem who were exiled in the land of Babylon.

31 And it came to pass, therefore, that this record of Moses was again sealed by Shaphan, the father of Lehi, after the order of Josiah, the king of Judah, for the posterity of Israel, and his seed, as set forth in the record of Lehi, for insomuch that his writings were hidden by him and his brethren, in a cave that lay between the mountainous plain of Meara, east of Sidon, and which was later required of Lehi to bring with him to this land of promise.

32 And it came to pass, when Lehi was commissioned, that when he was overpowered by the Spirit of the Lord, he was shown the sealed book of Moses, which he would have to protect, and that he was required to read his pages, thus coming to understand that which his father Shaphan had read years before to King Josiah concerning the destruction of Jerusalem, when he rent his garments before the prophecies described by the great Moses, which were to occur in all ages until the coming of the Messiah, and after Him, to the consummation of the fullness of times. Thus, with the other records on the brass plates from the beginning to Jeremiah, they were required by the Lord that Lehi should bring them from Jerusalem to this land of promise[1]. [1] RLDS 1Nephi 5:262-264; 1Nephi 1:9-12 / LDS 1Nephi 19:21-23; 1Nephi 1:11-13

33 Nevertheless, over time, the very book of the law, except for the sealed book of Moses' prophecies, had been transcribed in many brass books with a wise purpose of the Lord for the days of King Benjamin, which were distributed among the priests of the people of the Nephite nation, that they might remember the law of the Lord, and might teach the people to keep themselves holy before the heavens.

34 For this reason, it was that my father, Mormon, summed up among the two books of Moses, only the one that had been sealed and which had never been revealed to the children of the covenant because of their iniquities[1]. In turn, only those who truly believed and sought to know the mysteries of God, and received Him, received this knowledge, however, it was forbidden to divulge them[2]. [1] RLDS D&C 22:16 / LDS Moses 1:23 | [2] RLDS Alma 9: 15-21 / LDS Alma 12:9-11

35 And now, that record which in ancient times had been sealed by the great prophet Moses, is summed up in these sealed plates of Mormon, to be revealed only at the appointed time of the Lord.

36 In addition to the *Sealed Book of Moses*[1], there is the record of the *Acts of the Three Nephites*[2], written by Jonah, one of the sons of Nephi, who had been chosen by Jesus to be the chief disciple of the twelve whom He called[3]; also, there is a summary of the *Prophecies of Samuel* the Lamanite, which were fulfilled among my people, written by Nephi, at the command of Jesus[4] for the purpose of reminding the people of the covenant in the last days, before the coming of the Lord into His temple[5]. [1] RLDS D&C 22:24a-25 / LDS Moses

1:40-42; 2 Kings 22:8-20 | **(2) RLDS 3Nephi 13:29-30** / LDS 3Nephi 28:18 | **(3) RLDS 3Nephi 9:4-5** / LDS 3Nephi 19:4 | **(4) RLDS 3Nephi 10:34-41** / LDS 3Nephi 23:7-13 | **(5) RLDS D&C 38:5b; D&C 42:10c; D&C 65: 1d** / LDS D&C 38:22; D&C 42:35-36; D&C 65:5

37 Lastly, one-third of the record of the *Revelations of John*[1], written by the three Nephites, for insomuch that they saw these things revealed by an apostle of the Lord, whose name was John, when they were caught up and transfigured before the throne of God were shown unto them all things unspeakable from the mysteries of Heaven[2]; but because of the commandment which they received in heaven, to keep this knowledge sealed, they did not report it because they ministered among all the inhabited earth, but recorded the things which they saw and heard to be revealed, when finally, these things begin to occur again among the sons of men[3]. **(1) RLDS Ether 1:113-114; 1Nephi 3:238 -251** / LDS Ether 4:16-17; 1Nephi 14:18-27 | **(2) RLDS 3Nephi 13:24-27** / LDS 3Nephi 28:12-15 | **(3) RLDS 3Nephi 13:28** / LDS 3Nephi 28:16

38 Lastly it was left for me, Moroni, to make a record of the ancient inhabitants who here on this earth came before us and who were dispersed in the course of the fall of that great tower, at the time when the Lord confounded the language of the people in the days of Nimrod, which are recorded in the record of the twenty-four plates found by the people of Limhi, among which, I gathered a part with the plates that were selected by my father, in relation to the record of this people which I called the people of Jared, for how much I briefly summarized his history as the book of Ether, who had been the last Jaredite prophet who existed on the face of the earth.

39 The other part, which regards the writings of the brother of Jared, which also appear in these twenty-four plaques selected by my father Mormon, had originally been made similarly to Nephite writing, in which one can read more than one word per character, which allows to occupy the full space of the plates, however, made according to the Jaredite writing. It was then that I, Moroni, compiled the remainder of these plates in Nephite writing, using them to transcribe the rest of the report in the same pattern, to which, the Lord commanded it to be clustered to the sealed records of my Father. However, I did it with a mixture of letters, both Nephite and Jaredite.

40 So I did according to what the Lord showed me, to remain some symbologies of His holy and sacred order among all the writing of this book, that in later days of times, will serve as signs to understand the power of that faith that I, Moroni, would like to show the world[1], but which will only be possible according to the decrees of the heavens, to be revealed only after the coming of Christ in His temple[2], when finally, men exercise their faith equal to that of the brother of Jared. [1] RLDS Ether 5:6-7 / LDS Ether 12:6} | [2] RLDS D&C 38:5b; D&C 42:10c; D&C 65: 1d / LDS D&C 38:22; D&C 42:35-36; D&C 65:5

41 Notwithstanding, although the writing of this record, which bears the name of the brother of Jared, being *The Book of Morian-Cumer*, should remain sealed, together with the rest of the *Revelations of John* in the sight of the seer when these things begin to occur, after the first seals are opened.

42 Being that among these few things that will be drawn from the first sealed set, before being every book put together in a later period of time, will be sufficient to awaken the faith in the followers of Christ who will proceed from this great and marvelous work that will take place when these things begin to take place among the covenant people in the fullness of times, that the Lord may stretch forth His hand for the last time, that He may redeem His people that are of the house of Israel.

43 Will happen then, that the Book of Mormon will be, as prophesied by the prophets, opened in three periods of time, to begin with the arrival of the time of the end, when then, the prince of darkness was ruling the earth in those days, but will have no power over this land of promise, so that there will be on this earth the opening of the first determined time and a light shine in the darkness forever upon the sons of men and from there on, many will seek true knowledge.

44 And having passed a thousand two hundred and ninety days since the continual sacrifice was removed before the altar, then, as regards the remnant of darkness, a light from distant lands will shine from afar on the holy people of God with the opening of the first seal, and a period of appointed times will begin, when many will be cleansed and whitened and approved, but the wicked will certainly continue to act wickedly, and none of them will understand, but the insightful will understand.

45 Blessed are those who will remain faithful until the arrival of the thousand three hundred and thirty-five days when the third and last book is opened by our Lord and our advocate together the Father, yea, Jesus Christ[1] - Amen! **[1] RLDS D&C 38:5b; D&C 42:10c; D&C 65: 1d** / LDS D&C 38:22; D&C 42:35-36; D&C 65:5

THE SEALED BOOK OF MOSES

CHAPTER 1

And these words were spoken unto Moses in the mount, whose name shall not be known among the children of men: and now I, Mormon, will make according to the Lord's command only a summary concerning the Priesthood of the Son of God, to the believers in the first set of books I wrote and that was open in the records of these plates which were compiled by me as being the Book of Mormon, for Moses bore testimony of this to the chosen nation of his time: but because of iniquity, it is not found among the children of men, for it was sealed by Moses, and in later days of time were concealed by the Levites in a place called the Most Holy, under the altar that sustained the ark of the covenant, when at last they were found before the destruction of Jerusalem and brought to this land of promise by our patriarch Lehi.

1 Now I, Mormon, I make an account of the records that were found in the days of Josiah king of Judah; of which the prophets of ancient times spoke, that these words would be sealed until the time of the end; for how much many would be tried and purified, so that the presumptuous in the faith will not be able to understand, coming to become stubble for the great burning of the last day; for behold, the Lord shall pour upon all the proud a spirit of deep sleep, and again, He will close the understanding of His priests, so that they shall walk like the drunken of Ephraim, staggering, but not of intoxicating drink, but by becoming drunk with the wine of obstinacy, in carrying out their own counsel, because of his hard heart condition by bearing in greatness the lofty crown which in former times was laid upon the house of Ephraim.

2 But those who are humble will be refined and purified as gold in the furnace of the smelter, and the Lord will purify the sons of Levi from all uncleanness, when Jesus Christ will come to His temple and refine them like gold in the furnace of the goldsmith for be precious, living ornaments in the temple of God in Zion¹. ⁽¹⁾ _{Malachi 3:1-3}

3 I do not therefore write all the things that have already been summarized and compiled by me, Mormon, in the book of Lehi, and which details everything in his record since his life in Jerusalem and the reasons that made him cross the great waters until he comes along with his family to this land of Promise.

4 I do, however, give a reliable account of the events that began to occur in his days in Jerusalem concerning this sealed book of the great Moses.

CHAPTER 2

Hilkiah, the high priest, was appointed to the restoration of the temple by Josiah, king of Judah, in the days of Shaphan, the scribe secretary and soferim of all the languages that were around the land of Israel: the son of Azalias and the father of Ahikam, Elasah, which was later called by God by the name of Lehi, short for Eliashib, meaning "through whom God restores," and Gemariah and Jaazaniah. During the restoration of the temple, Hilkiah finds the own "book of the law of Jehovah, and together a scroll sealed by the signet ring of Moses himself hidden under the ark in the temple by the first Levites." Hilkiah delivers both the books he found to Shaphan, who reads the sealed manuscript to the king. Upon hearing the reading of the book, King Josiah rends his garments because of the abominations foretold in his record, which for fear that one of them would occur in his day, he sends to Huldah, the prophetess master of the school of the prophets, a delegation led by

the high priest Hilkiah, to inquire of the Lord, in the king's name,
concerning the prophecies predicted from beginning to end of all
things concerning this world, found in that record which was sealed,
if one of them was destined to happen in his day.

1 And it came to pass in the eighteenth year of the reign of Josiah,
king of Judah, that Hilkiah, the high priest, the son of Shallum, and
the father of Azariah, began the reformation of the temple under the
command of the king. In the course of these days, king Josiah sent
Shaphan, the son of Azalias, the son of Meshullam, to the house of
the LORD, saying: go to Hilkiah, the high priest, to gather all the
money from his hands which the people brought into the house of
the Lord. And take charge of delivering into the hands of the masters
of work, so that they distribute it to the workers in charge; to the
carpenters, and to the builders, and to the masons; and that we may
buy timber and hewn stones to repair the house of the LORD our
God, as it is commanded by the king of Judah.

2 It happened then, that the king's company came to the Temple,
supervised by Shaphan the father of Lehi, whom the high priest
Hilkiah said: See, I found the book of the law of Moses in the house
of the Lord, for how much is together to him, a part of the parchment
that remains sealed by Moses' own ring of seal. And Hilkiah gave
the book to Shaphan, for that he himself might research; and, for a
period of three days thereafter, stopping only to eat and rest, he read
them all completely.

3 It occurred after this, that Shaphan hastened to stand before the
king, first exposing to Josiah the answer regarding the expenses,
taxes concerning the restoration of the temple, saying: Your servants
gathered the money that was asked of the people, and delivered it
into the hands of those who have positions of supervision in the
work, which are in charge of the restoration of the house of the Lord.

31

4 It happened then, that Shaphan, the scribe, told the king, that Hilkiah the high priest delivered into his hand the lost book of Moses. And so he read it before the king, pausing and reasoning with him through what they understood of the writings they had of Moses and the prophets, and did so for days thereafter until they had finished reading in their entirety.

5 And it happened that, when the king heard the words of the book of the law, and subsequently as regards the sealed part of the manuscript of Moses, he tore his own garments, because among them were prophecies foretold by the Lord to Moses concerning all things related to the Priesthood of the Son of God and the consequences that fall upon the people of the covenant whenever the Elders of the house of Israel disrespect their investiture to the priestly position.

6 And the king commanded Hilkiah, the high priest after the house of Aaron, and Ahikam the son of Shaphan, and Achbor the son of Michaiah, and Shaphan the scribe of the king, and Asaiah the king's servant, saying: Since not we have a priest in our midst according to the order of Melchizedek, go ye even unto Huldah the prophetess, the wife of Shallum, the man of the cleaning of the garments of the temple, and inquire of the Lord for me, and for the people, and for all Judah, concerning the words of this book that was found; for great is the wrath of Jehovah, which is kindled against us; for how much our fathers did not heed the law of the Lord concerning the covenants received in the most holy order of the priesthood of God, the order of His Son, whose image reflected among His elect on earth is in the order of the priesthood of Melchizedek, for to do according to all that is written in the book Sealed of the law of Moses, in regard to this higher priesthood, so that we may be ready to receive it and so that it may remain with us, that we are children of the covenant and not only among the prophets appointed directly by God, but that every man of the house of Judah find yourself worthy to port it.

7 It happened then, that the high priest Hilkiah, proceeding from the house of Aaron; together with Ahikam and Achbor; Shaphan and Asaiah, they went to Huldah, the prophetess[1], the wife of Shallum, the son of Tikvah, the son of Haras, whose lineage was in designated of supervising the ones in charge of the garments of the Levites, and your he house was in the second part of the city, between the street that was designated to the washers and dyers of the priestly garments. [1] 2Kings 22:14

8 It happened then, that when they told Huldah these things, she said to them: Thus saith the Lord, the God of Israel, tell the man that hath sent you unto Me, behold, I will bring evil upon this place, and upon the inhabitants thereof, to know all the words of the book that were read to the king of Judah, for how much they have forsaken Me, and have burned incense to other gods, and they provoked Me, the Lord; who brought them out of the land of Egypt out of the house of the slaves, to make them a strong and mighty nation among the sons of men, for how much they were faithful to My laws, which in the days of old I gave the house of Israel.

9 But now, behold, My wrath is kindled because of all the works of your hands; and My wrath is kindled against this place, as it like never before, and it shall not be quenched until every nation is scattered unto the four corners of the earth. Nonetheless, so shall ye say to the king of Judah: Thus saith the Lord God of Israel, concerning the words which thou hast heard, for how much your heart was tender and humbled before the Lord your God when you heard the account of My servant Moses, who foresaw all things concerning this world and its inhabitants in a single instant, and can record the things that were to come to take place against this place because they do not endure the most holy order of My priesthood, which is according to the order of My Son, for how much was taken from you from the days of Moses My chosen servant, and they sought him no more in his manner of life, accepting with haughtiness a minor priesthood in relation to things that has reserved for them, but they have not been able to endure them to this day.

10 These are the days when I lift up My hand against its inhabitants, that there may be desolation and cursing among them that profess to be My priests in the land which I have assigned to your ancestors. But as for thee, O king of Judah, for how much you ripped your garments, and you cried before of Me the Lord, that also I will not abandon you completely, and behold, I, the Lord will gather you to your ancestors, and thou shalt be brought to thy grave in peace, and thine eyes shall not see all the evil that I will bring upon this place.

CHAPTER 3

Having been Moses caught up from the Principle, saw the angel Ahiah become miserable and propose to himself that all humanity would also be miserable just as he, and with that, began to lie and deceive the first parents of mankind. Eve and Adam succumb under the influence of this evil being that was expelled of heaven. Adam receives the priesthood of the Son of God, and with him the law of the priesthood and the promise about his righteous seed after him. Abel fulfills the requirements required by law, for how much Cain is induced for priestly tricks and commences false worship among his fellow men. Abel becomes the first prophet to seal with blood his work on earth. Seth is born and spreads the gospel and the priesthood through his offspring.

1 It so happened, that Moses was caught up on a mountain extremely high and came to Mount Zion in the Heavenly Jerusalem[1], and obtained knowledge of all things that were from the beginning, began to record what he saw and heard in the Sealed Book that was found by Hilkiah together with the book of the law in the days of Josiah king of Judah, which Lehi brought into this land beyond the sea, in order to preserve its record for future generations of priests of the holy order of the Son of God in the final part of the fullness of times[2]. [1] **RLDS D&C 22:1** / LDS Moses 1:1; **Hebrews 12: 20-23** | [2] **RLDS D&C 22:24a-25; 1Nephi 6:3** / LDS Moses 1:40-42; 1Nephi 19:23; **2Kings 22:8-20**

2 It was then that Moses passed to be in a great universal meeting, in which Ahiah, the angel whose name means "brother of Jehovah," greater leader who covered in his expansion the class of anointed cherubim — chief commander of the flaming stones, until the day he was deposed from his office and the supervision of heavenly visits to the sons of man, was delivered to the angel Gabriel, who commanded them for by the too much generations of Israel, when they were walking by the circuit of the heavens, which chariots of fire visited the prophets of God[1], full of wisdom and proceeding from the highest caste of the order of the stars d'alva, had full access to Mount Zion until the day he overturned the old covenant and vehemently accused the Great Jehovah of usurping the rights of free will in all beings created by Him in the vast expanse of the universe, for how much he himself came seeking to destroy free will of man from the beginning. [1] **Daniel 8:16; 9: 21; Luke 1:19: Job 22:14; Ezekiel 28:13-17; 2 Kings 2:11-12; 6:15-17**

3 And so, because he had been full of pride and vanity, assumed an air of grandeur and came to desecrate his own wisdom by supposing in his heart that he would be accepted by God in the highest and immaculate cradle of creation, after arousing appreciation of a vast multitude of followers, first of those whom he led astray in the heavens and now on earth, and so he longed to return to the holy mountain of meeting, and to take his place among the council of the heavens, which are above the holy angels, in the likeness of God[1], but beneath the sovereign Lord, the Almighty, which can not

35

overrule the ordinance established by Him in the heavens, of that the dominions of the earth would be in subjection to his son Ahiah, when then it even before the foundation of the world that was given the dominions of the Kingdom of mankind, and with that, he came to be in Eden, the garden of God[2]. [(1)] Isaiah 14: 13-14 | [(2)] Ezekiel 28:13

4 Being that man had been created in the image of God, reflecting in itself its divine attributes, namely: love, wisdom, creative potential and justice, and had also been created according to its likeness, thus obtaining characteristics similar to the image of its creator, coming to be an immortal creature, for how much were subject to themselves all creatures that move in heaven, on earth, and in the sea, but they had been commanded to fertilize and fill the earth and to expand the boundaries of Eden.

5 But it came to pass that Ahiah, when he sought to do that which was evil before God, was cast out of the highest and immaculate cradle of the heavens[1]. Yea, from the holy mountain of God, to heavenly Zion[2]. However, he had not yet been expelled from the heavenly realms, since he periodically made himself present at the universal meetings in order to present a report of his administration concerning this world which was under his dominion[3]. [(1)] RLDS Genesis 3:4 - IV / LDS Moses 4:3 | [(2)] Isaiah 14:12 | [(3)] Job 1:6-12; 2:1-6

6 Therefore, it was at the beginning of human history on earth, that after falling from his high position in the heavens, he became wretched before the children of God, and thereby proposed himself in subjecting all humanity to being unable to fully enjoy its free will and thus condemn them to the same misery and decay that had been condemned.

7 So that old serpent went on to deceive his brethren who lived with him in the heavens, and so soon became an opponent to God's plan for this world. It happened then that he went on to deceive the first human couple still in Eden, the paradise of God, coming to become the father of every lie, and so was called devil.

36

8 It was then, after Adam and Eve had succumbed to the wiles of the devil, that God proceeded to curse them, for before that they lived on a higher level on the spiritual plane. Though they were made of the dust of the earth, in Eden they were clothed with spirit and therefore immortal, but as soon as they sinned, God clothed them with mortal skin[1], therefore were cursed to suffer in the inclemency of time, pain, sweat and all sorts evils that are subject to mortal flesh. [1] **RLDS Genesis 2:10-13 IV** / LDS Moses 3:8-9; 4:27

9 However, the Father of tender mercies provided a means of redemption by which the children of Adam could return to their initial glory and again have full communion with God as they had in the beginning — This providence being the very Priesthood of God, that is according with the order of His son, being therefore called at the beginning of all times the priesthood of the Son of God.

10 Therefore, the gospel became the way for all to return to God, the scriptures of the holy prophets are the iron rod extended along this trajectory that intertwine through a dense mist of darkness, being the priesthood is the safe guide which lamp to light the way in the darkest night and keep us on the right course until we reach the tree of life, which is in the paradise of God beyond the thresholds of this mortal existence, and whose fruits correspond to the full happiness of attaining the reward of eternal life.

11 And as soon as God had cast out the man of Eden, putting cherubim of guard and a flaming sword around to keep the way of the tree of life, then the Lord provided this priesthood to man in order to choose between good and evil, otherwise, without the priesthood, man's way will be tortuous and his thoughts and inclination of his heart will be sensual and devilish most of the time.

12 Since these words concerning this priesthood of the Son of God, are those that the Lord told Moses that they are pure and true, and that they are not to be shown to anyone until the Lord orders a Moses in the last days, that he may reveal these words only to those who believe[1]. [(1)] RLDS D&C 22:24a-25; 2Nephi 2:32-35 / LDS Moses 1:40-42; 4:32; 2Nephi 3:17

13 And in this all the wisdom of God is manifested, for behold, all things were made according to the wisdom of Him that knoweth all things.

14 And if Adam and Eve had not transgressed, then they would have remained in the garden of Eden in an immortal state and yet would be with their perceptions wrapped in the innocence of the spirit, which would not allow them to have children and would never have joy because they did not know misery; not being able to decide for themselves the way of goodness because they did not know evil.

15 But Adam fell, fulfilling the requirements of the Father, to be fruitful and to fill the earth with his offspring, and the priesthood of the Son of God exists to make the people of the earth come to understand the plan of salvation and allow the children of the man to know how to wait for the Son of God, who will come in the fullness of time to redeem from the fall those who believed in Him in order to become free from the yoke of sin and death, so that they may return again to the presence of the Father[1]. [(1)] RLDS 2Nephi 1:105-118; Alma 9:64 / LDS 2Nephi 2: 19-26; Alma 13:2

16 However, since the sin of Adam resulted in the degeneration of the divine nature in man, so now, with his mortal and fallen nature, no descendant of Adam would have strength to resist the wiles of the devil, for how much live in the world of humanity. That is, in disobeying God the Father, Adam subjected all his offspring under the influence of Satan. With this, men would be condemned to the bondage of sin and death forever.

17 It was then that God proposed to Adam that He would provide a deliverer from the bondage of sin and death, "the designated seed," and beside that promise, God appointed Adam to be the first Priest according to the order of His Son, because the gospel began to be preached from the beginning, being declared by holy angels sent

from the presence of God to Adam, and by His own voice and by the gift of the Holy Spirit.

18 And so all things pertaining to the priesthood, including the high priesthood of the holy order of His Only Begotten, were confirmed upon the head of Adam by a sacred ordinance, and a decree was established in heaven and sent forth to remain in the world until the end[1]. **[1]** RLDS Genesis 5:44-45 Inspered Version JS / LDS Moses 5:59

19 In its turn, God uttered the following sentence upon Satan and the church of God in all the times predetermined by Him among his offspring, that is, those who take the side of Satan against God and his rule on earth and the seed of the priesthood of God, those to whom, under the promise of a covenant, they would receive the proper authority of the Son of God under the command and rule of the designated seed who will bruise his head by the following promise: "I will put enmity between you and the woman, between your offspring and his offspring, and He will bruise your head, and you will bruise His heel[1]." **[1]** RLDS Genesis 3:21 Inspered Version JS / LDS Moses 4:21

20 Therefore, no man can free himself from this yoke of slavery and death without the help of those who bear the priesthood of the Son of God. This Priesthood, which will be repeatedly attacked and confused by the power of Satan and his seed throughout the history of God's people. On the other hand, the 'designated seed' not to come from the corruptible seed of Adam, as it is with the members that make up this priesthood laid upon Adam and his righteous seed after him. Rather, it is necessary that its conception be accomplished by the power of the Holy Spirit through the immaculate womb of a virgin who is not tainted by concupiscence that affect the thoughts of the fleshly men.

21 It happened then, that I Mormon, for how much transcribed these words from the sealed record of Moses, that the voice of the Lord calling me said: Like a child on the lap, the dispensation of Adam could not fully understand these words of mine, but as the child grows and develops more fully, it becomes able to have the understanding of information that could not before be understood. Similarly, the purpose of My words in regard to My offspring involves a gradual understanding of times, in which, I the Lord, I will give the children of man, line by line, a little here and a little there, and blessed they will be, those who listen to My precepts, because they will get more[1]. [1] RLDS 2Nephi 12:36-38 / LDS 2Nephi 28:30

22 And, behold, I, the Lord, will conclude a series of covenants proceeding from Me to the children of man who will reveal many details with the unfolding of the dispensations, which will be fully understood in this period of time, in which this message, sealed by My servant Moses, is revealed in the eyes of My people in the last days.

23 Of course, the covenant I made with Adam and his righteous seed after him is sufficient assurance that I, the Lord, will keep My promises. Nevertheless, on many occasions, I God, I will kindly strengthen the validity of My covenants with the children of Adam, for how much I will have to redeem from his descendants a righteous man who is willing to keep My commandments.

24 These inviolable agreements of the everlasting gospel of My Only Begotten, give to you, mortal and fallen men, an even more solid base to trust in My words.

25 It was then that Cain, the firstborn of Adam, enduced by the cunning of the devil, began to create dogmas concerning the "designated seed", so that their symbols would serve as signs for the future generations of the sons of Adam, with the purpose of generating hope for a future restoration of what had been lost by his parents in Eden.

26 Because of the divine decree imposed on the descendants of Adam, that the soil had been cursed and that man would have to work hard so that, with the sweat of his face, he would reap his reward, Cain proposed then, that the fruits of the earth would be the symbol of the designated seed, and every time one was going through the painful process of plowing, sowing and cultivating the soil, he would be aware symbolically of the promised descendant and remember the cursed state of the children of man.

27 But, at the end of the work with the gratification of the harvest, the children of Adam should, in accordance with the dogmas taught by Cain, burn some fruits in the field to fulfill the word of God, "as the purpose of always remembering his promised descendant".

28 In this way, then, according to the precepts of Cain, similar to what happens with the crop, that after much labor brings its reward, in the end, the children of Adam would have their reward through "the appointed seed".

29 Abel, on the other hand, as he had since childhood the craft of gathering together in flock a reasonable number cows and sheep and birds in order to facilitate their tasks of milking milk every day and having eggs for food and wool for making blankets and clothing, did not come to know the field, and with that, put in controversy the sacred ordinances imposed by Cain to the future descendants of Adam.

30 Moreover, as the prophecy mentions that the serpent's offspring would injure the heel of the offspring of the promise, Abel "concluded" that this should be a bloodshed on the part of "the designated seed", for in the original of his Edenic dialect, God's correct pronouncement to the serpent would be to "bleed the heel", rather than to hurt, and for this reason Cain went unnoticed when he formulated his dogmas upon prophecy. With this in mind, Abel proceeded to formulate doctrines based on the original context described by his father Adam in the Edenic language, which would be to the nation of Israel in the days when Moses described this account, the equivalent of the word Sacrifice, which means, "Office of bleeding", already in the original of the language spoken by the

Hebrews in his day, Sacrifice, means bleeding, whence comes the word which, I, Mormon know in the Nephite language as being "sacrament". That is, the sacrament traces the will of the Lord from the beginning of time in order to always remember the designated seed, Jesus Christ.

31 Because of this, it came to pass that Abel, fulfilling the requirements of prophecy, and therefore, the requirements of the law, found it improper to offer fruits of the field as a sacrifice to God, just as Cain had proposed, because in the days when God commanded Adam to offer sacrifices on an altar, the angels who visited him said that it should be done as a symbol of the sacrifice to be made from the Only Begotten of the Father[1], and that only a blood sacrifice could in fact symbolically foreshadow this ceremony "with the purpose of always remembering" the future shedding of blood by the "designated seed" who would be wounded for the benefit of all men. [1] **RLDS Genesis 4:6-7 - IV** / LDS Moses 5:6-7

32 In turn, it was man himself, starting with Cain, who came to frame dogmas in order to reconnect his symbologies with the remembrance of a divine promise.

33 It happened then, that God was pleased with Abel's offer and rejected that of Cain's, because he knew that this approval would result in the sequel that Adam's descendants would give in observing that ordinance, which foreshadowed the correct understanding of the designated seed, and thus they would not observe the deceit proposed by Cain.

34 Because the children of man need symbols to remain faithful to the command of God, the Lord, then, accepted the most coherent and faith-filled dogma in the content described in the words of His prophecy. Therefore it was said "That by faith Abel offered God a better sacrifice than Cain. And by his faith he obtained the approval of God as a righteous man, and God himself approved of his offers".

42

35 It happened then, that the priesthood of the Son of God was full in Abel, but diminished in its fullness with each passing day on Cain, and with this, Cain himself came to the conclusion that the Lord looked with appreciation at the offerings of his brother while rejecting the fruits delivered as an offering to Lord by his own hands.

36 Cain, therefore, was incited by the devil and enticed of envy while anger seized his senses. Because Cain began to plan a way to interrupt Abel's life.

37 Abel, in turn, justified the plan of salvation through the promised descendant, the designated seed, and through proper observance correct of the ordinance to remember that promise.

38 It was then that the Lord sought out Cain through an angel sent to him from God to ease the wrath that nourished his heart. The Messenger then told him that God the Father had not rejected him when He showed favor to his brother's offering, but He was sad that there was envy and hatred in his heart. Then the Lord asked him the reason for his wrath, and so soon made him understand that the things that further him away from his Creator, were not in themselves their wrong form of worship, and the deceitful institution of their created ordinances with his precepts of earthly man, and that it would not be for this reason that God the Father would cease to hear his prayers, but his erroneous form of worship only removed the power of the priesthood which Adam had placed upon his head, just as he also laid upon Abel's head, who had been able to comprehend the mystery of the sacrament through an atonement for blood, which was to foreshadow the sacrifice of the descending fiancé, for whose painful ceremony it is required for a priestly human representative to raise his hand to take life, whose gift only God can give, and thus having to avail himself of death in an ordinance from the old covenant that would make them reflect in the shed blood of an innocent animal, and with this, the man who watched that helpless bloodied animal, writhing in agony for the purifying himself from his sins, would have to understand in his heart for the purpose of "always remembering" the future action proposed by the promised descendant, yea Jesus Christ.

39 For, it was so ordained in the heavens, that the power of divinity from the priesthood of the Son of God among the sons of Adam, can only be maintained among men in the flesh by a strict observation of their ordinances on earth[1]. [(1)] RLDS D&C 83:3b-3c / LDS D&C 84:19-21

40 However, what made Cain stay aloof from God were the feelings contrary to the star that shines in the Dawn[1], which allowed them to take root in his heart and, finally, the full power of the priesthood lost its effectiveness to the opposition of the feelings who grieve the Spirit of God[2], pushing it away from their hearts. [(1)] 2Peter 1:19; RLDS Alma 16:160-163 / LDS Alma 32:34-35 [(2)] Ephesians 4:30

41 Such sentiments led him to deliberate sin when Cain finally rejected the counsel of God and set out to murder his brother. Thus, such feelings were contrary to these, which were once instituted by God to be sentiments that govern the highest celestial characteristics in the sons of Adam, and with them, righteous men in the flesh, can control the priesthood of God[1]. [(1)] RLDS 1Nephi 5:144-147/ LDS 1Nephi 17:45

42 These same feelings were established even before the foundation of the world to interact with the human sensibility, so that the children of men, even without the priesthood of God, can identify in midst of their fleshly nature those good feelings that proceed from God to guide them in the way of justice and charity[1]. [(1)] RLDS D&C 9:3b-3c / LDS D&C 9:8

43 But, since Satan has interposed in the human heart an emotional parallel that leads the children of men to confuse the noble divine feelings with the mere desires of their hearts, men end up exchanging the excellence of right motivation with regard to the pure sentiments derived from the fruits of the Holy Spirit that is in the gospel of the Only Begotten of the Father, by a fleeting sense of greatness in his way of feeling and thinking, which ultimately

44

corrupts his magnificence before the heavens, desecrating his true nature in a fallen and degrading condition that will lead man to a continual endeavor to satisfy his need for happiness, by a deception designed by the enemy in their hearts[1]. [1] Proverbs 28:26; Jeremiah 17:9-10

44 However, true happiness comes from within, and proceeds from the light emanating from the Holy Spirit and not from things that temporarily fill the void that causes men to lack true knowledge in their way of feeling[1]. [1] Luke 24:32; Galatians 5:22-24

45 It so happened that God made Cain to know what Satan knew beforehand, that his offering would be rejected, and would rejoice with it. Further, God told many things to Cain concerning his errors, and warned him about his course, and that he would be accepted again by the Lord, if only he would withdraw from nourishing these evil feelings and return to do good in relation to his brother Abel[1].

[1] Galatians 5:25-26; RLDS Genesis 5:9 - IV; D&C 9:3c-3d / LDS Moses 5:23; D&C 9:8-9

46 But Cain loved Satan more than God because Satan promised to serve his personal interests, but in exchange Cain would have to make his brothers worship him, engendering secretly the Devil's deception together with the truth of God in order to appear as close to the precepts that the children of Adam had received to identify the truth of the Father[1]. [1] 1John 2:7-8, 24-27

47 And so Satan proposed to work through Cain great signs and wonders to deceive everyone as possible, and to gain an active power among the children of men that equates with the priesthood of the Son of God, which was given first to Adam and his righteous offspring after him, because just as happened to Cain, all those who choose to follow the precepts of Satan will also lose the power of the priesthood, and with this, Satan will have full power over the children of men who are deceived by their rise and priestly deception.

48 It happened, then, that Satan swore loyalty to Cain, just as Cain swore by his own life, that neither he nor his brethren who would rise after him in the priesthood order proposed by Satan, would reveal the secrets of this order to the righteous sons of Adam. With this, Satan proposed to Cain to deliver Abel into his hands and to take possession of all his flocks and goods and to make him supreme master in the order of the priesthood Mahan, whose source of power comes from the Devil. However, Cain would have to shed Abel's blood in confirmation of the covenant established with Satan[1]. [1]

RLDS Genesis 5:14-18 IV / LDS Moses 5:29-33

49 Happened then, that after Cain deliberately disobeyed the guidance of God and consequently killed Abel, that God cursed him saying: While Abel justifies My plan in the land to have righteous descendants of the priesthood in relation to My offspring, you, Cain, justify the offspring of the original serpent, Satan the devil, for he became a perdition to the sons of men, for he is wiser than you to deceive you, because this one was full of wisdom before there was Eden, because he existed even before the foundation of the world[1].

[1] RLDS Genesis 5:10 IV / LDS Moses 5:24; **Ezekiel 28:12-17**

50 And so, from the dawn of time, Cain and Abel foreshadow the two priestly castes in relation to the wicked priests of the Mahan class and the righteous men of the priesthood of the Son of God, that exist from the beginning and will exist until the end of time. Just like me, Moses, could see with my own eyes the similar power of the Mahan priests from Egypt in relation to the priesthood power of the Son of God resting upon me[1]. [1] Exodus 7: 10-13, 20-22; **RLDS Genesis 6:7 IV /**

LDS Moses 6:7

51 And thus said the Lord: this is the sacred Secret that you, Moses, must keep sealed in this book that I made you write after that My people Israel harden the heart for want of the right spirit, that are feelings that in times past, I the Lord, gave through the Holy Spirit so that My people would observe My power acting within themselves, in relation to My priesthood, when I gave you the key to this knowledge to teach them clearly in the desert, so that they could have full communion with Me the Lord, and that it is only through the use of the right feelings which they should have in their hearts that it is possible to make use of the attributions derived from the priesthood authority of the Son of God, and that there is no other way of subduing the powers of the heavens and establishing the "Order of Enoch", except in accordance with the invocation of the high sentiments which pertain to that order[1]. [1] **RLDS D&C 83:3b-4a** / LDS D&C 84:19-23

52 Know therefore, Moses, that before I take you out of the midst of this people because of the hardness of their hearts, as I will also take away the holy priesthood from them, that I, the Lord, will cause to remain with this people only the priesthood lesser and preparatory among them, until My descendant comes.

53 You must, therefore, summon a class from the Levites, whose office must be from generation to generation, in order to conceal from the sons of men this manuscript, until I, the Lord, raise in due time, a Moses like unto thee, and he will make known the words of this book to those who will be willing and ready to attend to this commitment with Me the Lord, and thus this knowledge will again be within the reach of the children of men, among all who believe[1].

[1] **RLDS D&C 22:24b; D&C 83:4a-4d; 2Nephi 2:32-35** / LDS Moses 1:40-42; D&C 84:23-27; 2Nephi 3:17

54 Behold, you are well aware of this agitation in your mind, My servant Moses, and you know how difficult it is to recognize the feelings of light amidst this stupor of emotions coming out of darkness, which tends to prevent the children of men to identify feelings originating from light and truth, for how much it was required that you should invoke Me, the Lord, in your afflictions, when you were with the people among the mountains and were surrounded by the carriages of Pharaoh and the waters of the sea, and so the people were filled with uncertainty, and the stupor of fear and doubt suddenly came to occupy their thoughts, and as soon as they left out the feelings of faith and gratitude that until then, filled their hearts.

55 Immediately they lost out their convictions of serving unconditionally to Me the Lord, with all their heart, soul and understanding. But as for you, Moses, you marveled at My previous deed and remembered My work in the land of Egypt and kept full hope in your countenance, to that I, the Lord, would save them, seeking in you the highest feelings that may exist in earthly man, who bring forth the power of My priesthood among the children of men in the flesh, and when you had compassion on My people, which was about to perish in the hand of Pharaoh, you found yourself then in full condition of summoning My presence, not in words, because My name can not be pronounced by the human mouth, but in your heart, invoking the feeling that prefigures My whole being, which you could only understand in the realm of human understanding as being the most sublime and elevated feeling that there is, yea, of the unconditional love.

56 For whosoever shall call upon My name shall be saved, and so shall it be in the last days among My people[1]. But how shall they call on Him whom they have not known, by whose name no mouth can pronounce? [1] Joel 2: 32; Zephaniah 3: 9

57 Now, this is the great mystery which I, Moses, must keep hidden from the world until the Lord finds it prudent to reveal it to the sons of men, for it is the key to operating the Holy Priesthood of the Son of God.

58 And, for the purpose of no one to usurp His name, it was that the priesthood in the days of Abraham was called the priesthood of Melchizedek. This was determined in ancient times, even in the days when it was known according to the order of Enoch in recognition of the high priesthood that dignified Enoch[1], and then, according to the order of Melchizedek, in honor of the great high priest who was Melchizedek when he reigned over Salem, obtaining double peace

48

under his rule, both in the position he held as king, and in the office of high priest[2]. [(1)] **RLDS D&C 76:5g** / LDS D&C 76:57| [(2)] **RLDS Genesis 14: 26-27 IV;** **Alma 10:7** / LDS Alma 13:14

59 It was, therefore, out of reverence for the name of God that this Holy Priesthood, according to the Order of the Only Begotten Son[2], which is found in the likeness of the Father and who, par excellence, received the same name as His. Yea, it is in Him that one fulfills the words directed to me Moses, by the great Jehovah, when said: Behold, I send an Angel before thee, to keep thee in the way, and to bring thee into the place which I have prepared. Beware of Him, and obey His voice, provoke Him not, for He will not pardon your trangsressions, for My name is in Him, and since no other angel has inherited a name like His, is therefore, as excellent as I AM[1]. [(1)] Exodus 23:20-21; Acts 4:12; Philippians 2:9; Hebrews 1:4

60 This is, therefore, the key to the priesthood and the mystery that will be sealed in this book until the time of the end, because there is nothing more sacred to be revealed to men in the flesh than this knowledge, that the name of God can be invoked in their hearts, and that one can not evoke the powers of the heavens in the holy priesthood of the Son of God, unless it be through sentiments derived from the love of the Only Begotten Son of the Father, each one correspondent to his ministry, because to some, as the Spirit leads, produce sundry feelings, which we call God's gifts[1]. [(1)] 1John 4:8; Romans 12:4-21; 1Peter 4:10

61 You can not, therefore, effect a single part of My work if there be not among you the sentiments derived from the gifts which correspond to a spark of Me, the Lord.

62 No, in no way can My people live the height of My priesthood in a united order, as it did in the days of Enoch, without the noblest and high feeling in their hearts, all derived from charity, which is the purest expression of the love of God among the children of men, much less you can effect any ministry, whether it be healing or powerful works without any of the feelings derived from this greater gift.

63 This, therefore, is the procedure among the various ministries which are in the priestly order of the Only Begotten Son, for no authorized representative in the sacred order of My priesthood can perform any miracle, such as healing, unless there is the gift of compassion in your hearts when they pray with hands on top of the sick.

64 Your action will be in vain if there is no corresponding feeling within you to do the work, whatever it may be.

65 This, therefore, is the secret sealed which must be hidden from future generations until Shiloh[1], in the meridian of times, comes, and an appendix demonstrative of the full power of My holy priesthood be given through Him to be revealed again in the final part of the fullness of times, when at last this book, which I command that you seal it, will be again exposed to the remnants of My people in the last days. [1] Genesis 49: 10 IV

66 Behold, I say unto you, Moses, for the purpose of registering in this book these My words, because the men to whom this record arrive, must be those who will erect Zion in the last days.

67 But, behold, to raise up Zion, there must be love among My people, just as you, Moses, loved the children of Israel unconditionally and hast encouraged them not to be afraid, but to stand firm in their faith in the Lord so that they might see salvation from Me.

68 And what else should I expect of a prophet, if not that he rather encourage My people to walk in their confidence as if they saw the Lord before their eyes?

69 It was then that I led you to this narrow strip of land between the mountains and the sea, because I, the Lord, do not work with the children of men except according to their faith.

70 And what is faith? — Behold, faith is the sum of all the feelings of trust that are in your hearts which nullify the feelings of fear and doubt as to My performance among those who are My elect.

71 It was then that I, the Lord, told him: "Because, Moses, you persist to cry out to Me when there is in you the full strength of My priesthood resting in your feelings? — Also, know that you have in your retreat the multitude of the children of Israel, that are one with you, Moses, even as thou art one with Me, the Lord.

72 It is up to you, therefore, to awaken this spark in the hearts of this people, which adds power in the unity of feelings, and I, the Lord, am talking about the church collectively, because when the unity coexists among you, then you become one in Me.

73 And yet I tell you: Your collective feelings united in a common goal will allow you, Moses, in the use of the attributions conferred upon the presidency of the high priesthood, to transpose all things to continue using your power with Me, provided there is unconditional love in you by this people, and if this people have faith in Me, the Lord, through you and your words, then no condition can be imposed on you by the elements of this world and then nothing will be impossible for you because of faith in the hearts, mind and strength of this people, which is one in Me the Lord.

74 Therefore, spread your hand over the sea, and with the strength of these sentiments which comes from compassion, free the winds that are locked in the floodgates of the heavens and cause the children of Israel to pass through the sea on dry ground[1]. [1] Exodus 14: 10-16

75 Happened then, following the story of our first parents, that after the death of Abel, Cain proceeded to take one of his brothers' daughters as wife for himself and they both loved Satan more than God, and thenceforward, along with many of his brothers, lived east of Eden, in a land that had first been inhabited by Nod, one of the first sons of Adam, where Nod settled with his offspring[1]. [1] RLDS

Genesis 5:13, 26 IV / LDS Moses 5:28; 41

76 Cain and his wife had sons and daughters, and he built a city and gave her the name of his son Enoch, and created them according to their veneration, so that their offspring had in the highest esteem this evil one who is Satan as being god; and the true God he taught his children that This one was a postulation of evil.

77 And it came to pass that one of the sons of Cain had many sons, and he became king of this city, and of his sons there was Irad from whom Mehujael proceeded, and from Mehujael came Methusael from whom Lamech was born, whom Satan incited to have two wives, Adah and Zillah, and with this, polygamy began among the sons of men, for Lamech had made a covenant with Satan, and to seal this covenant he offered the innocent blood of Gibeah, a righteous man from the lands of Havilah, where there is abundance of gold that is on the banks of the river Pison, and together with this agreement, Satan proposed that he take a second wife to satisfy the diabolical and sensual feelings that permeated the heart of Lamech[1]. [1] RLDS Jacob 2:36-37 / LDS Jacob 2:27-28

78 This Gibeah, in turn, was a righteous man among the sons of Adam, and he endeavored to preach repentance among the sons of Cain, from which Lamech improperly seized his ornaments of gold and precious stones, and took possession of his goods and animals, becoming the first thief among the sons of men and a murderer just as Cain, who also shed innocent blood to seal his covenant with Satan the Devil in the manner of the order Mahan, thus becoming a master of the order and lord of that great secret that had been given to Cain.

79 Irad himself had been summoned to serve Lamech, and he made him acquainted with his secrets, which he did not restrain, and proceeded to tell the sons of Adam about the disgusting things that came from Satan, whom he had for god, and that at last they imprisoned the children of men under a degrading and miserable condition, and so Lamech killed Irad, his brother, to keep their secret combinations among the priests of the order Mahan, which has existed since the days of Cain[1]. **(1) RLDS Genesis 5:26-37 IV** / LDS Moses 5:47-51

80 It was then in these days of abominations among the sons of men, when they no longer kept the commandments of God, and the priestly precepts of the order Mahan spread throughout all inhabited land, that God raised up a righteous offspring again for Adam, and he went on to call him by the name of Seth.

81 And when he was still a young man, God showed himself to Seth and commissioned him, and Seth gladly accepted his call to preach repentance among his brethren. It was therefore at the age of sixty-nine that Seth was ordained to the priesthood by his father Adam, when it was then proposed to establish among his descendants the order of this priesthood of the Son of God, having for basis of all directives which were revealed from heaven, and the sons of men knowing that this was the standard proposed by God from the beginning, that the presidency of high priesthood should be handed down from father to son, or to a righteous descendant of the promise, if there is no worthy heir to assume the place of his father in the highest office that exists in the hierarchy of the church.

82 Therefore, the priesthood presidency of the Son of God belongs rightfully to the literal descendants of the chosen seed, to whom the covenant promises have been and will be made, and this same order that has always existed, will exist until the end of the world. Therefore, Adam, the president of the high priesthood in his day, spread the gospel with Seth, and came to confer priesthood on Enos, son of Seth, when he was a hundred and thirty-four years old.

83 And God called Cainan, the son of Enos, by a messenger in the wilderness when he was forty years old, and he proceeded to preach repentance to the sons of Cain and the descendants of Adam, and after forty and seven years since God called him on one of his journeys to Shedolamak, was that Cainan came upon Adam preaching among the multitude of his descendants, and it was on this occasion that Adam ordained him to the priesthood[1]. [1] **RLDS Genesis 6:7 IV; D&C 104:18-21** / LDS Moses 6:7; D&C 107:40-45

84 And it came to pass, when Adam was nine hundred and twenty and seven years old, that he gathered together in a place called Adam Ondi Amman, and Enos, and Cainan, and Mahalaleel, and Jared, and Enoch, and Methuselah. All high priests of the holy order of the Son of God, and there bestowed the keys of his presidency on the head of Seth, being blessed by his father three years before Adam's death[1]. [1] **RLDS D&C 104:19a, 28a** / LDS D&C 107:42, 53

CHAPTER 4

In the days of Enos, "he began to call upon the name of Jehovah". Seth, Enos, Cainan, Mahalaleel, and Jared were preachers of justice. Enoch, still a young man, walks with God and sends a message of judgment against the wicked children of men. Enoch sees the spirits created by God and, as happened to Moses, he also sees innumerable worlds created by God and inhabited. The news of a seer spreads quickly. Enoch establishes the city of Zion, he foresees the coming of the Only Begotten Son and the restoration that will unite his people in a Zion in the last days; and the second coming; and the coming of heavenly Zion. God took them.

1 It happened then, that in the course of the story of Adam and his righteous offspring, after God showed himself to Seth and he came to offer to the Lord, through a higher knowledge than his brethren, an acceptable sacrifice just like the sacrifice of Abel. But more full of clarification of the gospel than any of the sons of Adam had previously understood[1]. [1] **RLDS Genesis 6:3 - IV** / LDS Moses 6:3

2 It happened that, for Seth, a son was born, and he gave the name of Enos, and it was at this time that the children of Adam again began to call upon the name of Jehovah in their hearts, and so it was said that in the days of Enos, they began to call on the name of the Lord[1], because it was at this time that these men began to relive the true feelings derived from the name of God in their way of feeling, bringing a rescue of the priesthood powers of the Son of God among brothers who began to share in common all things, including a language which was pure and virtuous, and this same priesthood and posture among the children of men will again be revived in the end times with the people of God in Zion[2], which will rise through the words of this book, and will restore to the people in the last days the dialect of a pure and immaculate tongue on the part of those who will invoke the Lord, not by the babbling of the impure human tongue, but by the spiritual dialect, when expressing the divine sentiments in the hearts of those who will ground the citizenship of Zion in themselves, for this is what will truly sustain the foundations of Zion in the last days, a people pure in heart[3]. [1] RLDS Genesis 6:4, 5 - IV / LDS Moses 6:4, 5 | [2] RLDS Genesis 6:6-7 - IV / LDS Moses 6:6-7 | [3] Zephaniah 3:9; RLDS D&C 94:5c / LDS D&C 97: 21

3 In turn, some descendants of the sons of Cain, in their own way, also began to verbally invoke the name of the God of Adam. However, they did so in an erroneous and profane manner, only by making use of a pronouncement from the human tongue, and with this they began to make for themselves idols of stones and wood, in order to worship Him. Subsequently they applied Jehovah's sub-names to their idols, by which they believed that they were thus, approaching God in worship.

4 And the priests who proclaimed it, had great dominion over the sons of Cain, who were the majority on the face of the earth. On the other hand, Seth, Enos, Cainan, Mahalaleel, and Jared, being preachers of justice, spread the gospel wherever they went, establishing congregations everywhere and teaching their followers the power that is the name of God, and were again aware that of the feelings derived from His name were the keys that control the priesthood power of the Only Begotten Son among men in the flesh, thereby nullifying the influence and power of Satan wherever they preached.

5 This, in turn, infuriated Satan in his heart, causing him to bring wars and bloodshed, where brother killed brother, and by means of secret combinations gave power to the emissaries of the order Mahan so that they prevented the other children of men to hear the message propagated by the righteous children of Adam, that, everywhere of inhabited earth, the good news of the everlasting gospel was being preached, which began to exist in the days when God left the holy priesthood of His Son upon Adam and his descendants so that all would turn to God again.

6 It was then, between that time period, in which men began to call upon the name of the Lord; and that the Lord blessed them, which Seth begat Enos; and taught his son Enos the ways of God. And in those days Satan exercised great dominion among men and was infuriated in his heart; and from then on came wars and bloodshed; and seeking power, the man's hand rose up against his own brother to provoke him to death because of secret works, and for this reason Enos and the rest of the people of God came out of the land called Sulon and inhabited a promised land to whom he gave the name of his own son, whom he called Cainan.

7 And Cainan lived according to the commandments of God, up until he begat Mahalaleel. And Mahalaleel begat Jared; And Jared lived according to the teachings of his fathers, and begat Enoch. And Jared taught Enoch to walk uprightly in all the ways of God.

8 And it came to pass that Enoch journeyed on the earth among the people preaching and exhorting them to repentance; and as he traveled, he began to lie down beneath a leafy olive tree on a

mountain of a certain elevation in the land of Cainan, which he from henceforth called Mount Zion, for it was in that place that the Spirit of God came upon him, and because it was there that he saw His holy myriads of angels, and from that time he erected a city, having in that place the center of worship of God, where he proposed to build a temple to the Lord, the first one that was built by men on Earth.

9 While he was in a vision, he could see the Lord coming from the heavens in the last days, and with His holy myriads, as the clouds cover the earth, execute His judgment upon all peoples of the world of mankind, and to condemn all the wicked for all the unrighteous deeds that they have done improperly before their eyes and for all the unrighteous things that sinners have done against their fellow men, for thus shall the wicked be in the last days, acting and speaking evil of their neighbor, and blaspheming against the very God who created them[1], for the man speaketh the things that are in his heart. [1] Jude 14, 15

10 The man of God, however, of his good feelings, external good things in uttering his words, while the bad man, of his bad heart, speaks only evil things. Then it was said to Enoch that men will also give account on the Day of Judgment for every worthless statement they make about their neighbor and about God; for by their deeds men will be declared righteous or unjust, and by their words, men will be freed or condemned[1]. [1] Matthew 12:32 - IV

11 Then a voice from heaven said unto him: Enoch, My son, prophesy unto this people, and command them to repent, for thus saith the LORD; I am wroth with this people, and My wrath is kindled against them; for their hearts hardened, and they cover their ears, that they might not hear My messengers, the prophets, and their eyes, that they might not see My work.

12 For behold, this people, who claim to be My people in the last days, draw nigh unto Me, and with their mouths and lips honor Me, but remove their heart from Me, and the fear of Me is taught according to the precepts of men and no more according to My sound doctrine — and for these many generations from the day that I have created them up until the fullness of time, they shall continually depart from Me, the Lord, and shall deny My statutes, and seek their counsel in the darkness, even as it is in thy days, My son Enoch; and in their own abominations they plan the murder, and keep not the commandments which I gave unto their father, Adam.

13 It is they who swear falsely, and by their own oaths bring death upon themselves; and a prison, I, the Lord, have prepared for the spirits of these sinners to remain imprisoned in an eternal course[1], for I am the Lord, I am the same, I have not changed, and I will never change, for My ways are eternal and unchanging, and this is the design of My hands until the day of final judgment, when then My Only Begotten proposed in himself, for a full administration in the full limit of the times I have designated, to release the captives in spiritual prisons, if they repent of their sins[2] and come to Me, the Lord their God and be delivered from captivity and death, when at the end the soul is restored to the body and the body to the soul[3]. [1]

RLDS D&C 2:1c / LDS D&C 3:2| [2] **RLDS Alma 19:69** / LDS Alma 41:6| [3] **RLDS Alma 19:58** / LDS Alma 40:23

14 And this is a decree which I have promulgated in the beginning of the world, of My own mouth, from its foundation; and by the mouth of My servants, I decreed it, just as it will be propagated in the world, from beginning to end, through My prophets, being therefore, imperative for My justice that men should be judged according to their works in the flesh[1], and there will be no resurrection while this earthly mortal body lives in corruption[2], until My Only Begotten come, and in Him men may repent of their sins.

[1] **RLDS Alma 19:66** / LDS Alma 41:3 | [2] **RLDS Alma 19:29; 19:67** / LDS Alma 40:2; 41:4

15 And so it has been given to man from the beginning a probationary time, until man accepts the righteousness of God, which is prefigured in the figure of His promised offspring, established even before the foundation of the world according to the plan of redemption, which can not be realized except in the face of the repentance of men in this probationary state which is the eternal course, without which men in the flesh would never attain knowledge of the plan of redemption and they would never repent of their sins. Therefore, if there were no eternal course established in opposition, but necessary to the plan of happiness, as eternal as the life of the soul, mankind could never repent and come to Me to save them[1]. [1] RLDS Alma 19:84, 94 , 98 / LDS Alma 42:4, 13, 16

16 And when he had heard these words, Enoch fell down before the LORD, and spake, saying: Why hath I found grace in thine eyes? I am only a boy and, behold, your people hate me because, unlike my father, I'm weak in the speech. So tell me, why have you chosen me as your servant to tell the people these things? And the LORD said unto Enoch: Go and do as I have commanded you, and no man shall smite thee. Open thy mouth, and it shall be full of wisdom, for I will give thee the words which thou shalt speak, and I will make thee mighty in thy judgments, for all flesh is in My hands; and I will do what seems right to you. For behold, I, the Lord, have found favor in the man you became, though be yet a boy. For there is in you all the good feelings which I esteem are the primordial tools of priests of the holy order of My Only Begotten.

17 What makes you pleasing to My eyes, because never before have I found in one man the fullness of My name engraved on his heart, just as there is within you, the feelings of Charity; Enthusiasm, Peace of the Spirit; Resignation to withstand adversities; Benignity; Compassion; Faith; Tenderness and Self-control. Believing that you will attain a higher kingdom with such gifts that are in you, seek to have with you a congregation of those who resemble you.

18 For if you can gather all the good feelings derived from My name into the men, women, and children of your congregation, then the sum of these attributes will be My reason to take you, because you bear in yourself the likeness of My Only Begotten, who is full of grace and power.

19 And because you have all these gifts within your heart, you will never walk alone, because I will always be with you, while you will walk with God in your ways.

20 For, behold, the feelings of My name that are in you are intimate; therefore I will justify all your words; and the mountains shall flee before thee, and the rivers shall stray from their course; and you shall abide in Me, that is, in My priesthood, for behold, I call upon My servant Adam, the first Priest of the holy order among men, to ordain you to the priesthood of My Only Begotten[1], and so obtain in you the fullness of My grace that already act in you through the faith that is in your heart. **[1] RLDS D&C 104:24a** / LDS D&C 107:48

21 Therefore, walk with Me. Now, however, anoint thine eyes with clay, and wash them; and thou shalt see. And so did Enoch, that which God commanded him. Happened then, as Enoch traveled by the eastern sea in the flaming carriages of the cherubim, that a vision opened before his eyes and the Lord led him through the many abodes that are in the vastness of the heavens, where Enoch was informed of the importance of the Name of God among the elect people of his day, and the gifts, which are sentiments derived from the sacred name to inhibit and drive away the powers of darkness among the children of men by the knowledge of His pure doctrine and the correct observance of His commandments.

22 God then made known to him the importance of His name, which was already being invoked in the hearts of those who heard the preaching of his ancestors but who did not understand the importance of using these gifts derived from the name of God, or in other words, the sentiments that flow from His Name, to obtain thereby, the victory over the influential powers of Satan, which are feelings coming from the darkness, opposed to the gifts of the Holy Spirit.

23 In order to evoke the many names of God, it is necessary to develop the gifts, therefore, the corresponding feelings for each one of them, and yet protect your hearts against the evil feelings that will be interposed in an uproar and stupor of thoughts.

24 Faith, in turn, grounds right feelings, nullifying the influence of opposing feelings, and this generates the strength of the priesthood within man, who in turn interacts in the physical world. And this is the way prepared from the foundation of the world, in which the Only Begotten Son shall come into the world, and glorify the name of the Father; giving His disciples knowledge of these things[1], preparing the way by which others may be partakers of this Gift, that they may have hope. And if you have only hope, so that your feelings can not be shaken, then you will have faith, and if you have this faith, then you have in yourself the keys to open or close all situations[2]. **[1]** **RLDS Genesis 6:44** / LDS Moses 6:42 | **[2]** **Hebrews 11:1; John 17:26; RLDS Ether 5:9-13** / LDS Ether 12:8-12

25 The names of God are fundamental so that we can know more about Him. Because they are an expression of the person of God within the children of men, reflecting their nature, importance and divine characteristics among our fellow men. God reveals Himself in us through their names, so that we are the representatives of His name on the face of the whole earth, and if you take the name of His Son, who is after the likeness of the Father, whose name equals to yours, then such names will lead you to know and admire His attributes, which are inseparable from His Person, and just as it was said to Enoch, man shall also walk with God, and being in this state of communion through the Priesthood or the grace of God in relation to women and other members of the covenant who were not called to the priesthood, but are filled with grace the likeness of the Only Begotten Son of the Father, the elements then, recognize the command of him who, acting in the name of His Son, through the feeling corresponding to the desired action, that is, to the divine stimulus within himself, then nothing will be impossible, but behold all things will be subject to him through faith and prayer.

26 However, Enoch was informed that to other men it was not lawful to know how to invoke the Almighty God in his day, and therefore he was forbidden to divulge this information to any other man or woman, except to those who showed themselves worthy of such merit within the covenant people. For in his days, that is, in the days of Enoch, this ineffable power, it was the key for the wicked to return their imagination inadequately to this Great Gift, the name of God, and thus to profane it without realizing the high attributes which derive from the name of the Most High, because they should never be evoked by a heart full of iniquities.

27 This sacred secret, made known to all men outside the covenant, would make the name of God a common evocation in the hearts of the children of men, which in the end would nullify their effectiveness even among their elect, and possibly among priests of His Order. For many, it would be questionable whether this is really real, or just an ordinary ordinance that is available to all, both to just and to unjust.

28 In these days, however, some of the holy sentinel angels, who were of the watchers class[1], who were designated from the beginning as heralds of God in regard to earthly affairs; and therefore they could materialize in carnal bodies, in the likeness of men, and to infiltrate among the sons and daughters of Adam, under the influence of Anaquiel, the person responsible for the plot that took place among the vigilantes who were corrupted, known among his fellows by Azazel, being the principal of those who abandoned their position that they obtained in heaven, they came to build for themselves great refuges, in which some of them, under the influence of Satan, had intercourse with the daughters of men, and in it have they brought forth seed; the giants of the land[2]. [1] Daniel 4:17, 23 |[2] RLDS Genesis 8: 6 - IV / LDS Moses 8: 18

29 Due to an agreement made between the Watchers[1], so that the angels who were rebellious would not come to imprison[2] the remaining vigilantes who remained in the land to fulfill their purpose among the children of men and that they would leave the covenant people in peace. [1] Daniel 10:11-13 | [2] Daniel 4:17, 23

30 So that even to this day, for how much Aaron separated by cast lots, two goats, one for Jehovah to atone for the sins of the children of Israel, and one for to hand over for Azazel[1], with the purpose of remembering the agreement of separation between the Sentinels. [1] Leviticus 16:8, 10

31 Thus, Aaron presents the goat that is appointed to Jehovah and will make him an burnt offering by the sin of men before God, but the goat appointed for Azazel must be brought alive before Jehovah to make atonement upon him in remembrance of the agreement between them, so that it may be sent into the wilderness for Azazel to remember this agreement.

32 For this reason it was decreed among the priests that "the man who sent the goat to Azazel should wash his clothes and bathe in water before returning to the camp; and only then can he enter among the children of Israel[1]." — This is because this man went to meet an evil angel and must purify himself spiritually and physically before returning to the congregation of the one God. [1] Leviticus 16:26

33 But, behold, the giants were obtuse, without much reasoning and, therefore, dependent on their parents. In turn, in order not to allow these men of great structure to become slaves of men by reason of their dementia, it was that the sentinel angels, who had been disobedient in abandoning their position with the Father[1], they began to use earthly men to build cities whose architecture was a representation of heavenly things. [1] Jude 6

34 So the men began to obtain from the watchers[1] the proper knowledge to mold the iron and to work their mixtures. Thus, they could forge all sorts of devices, from more resistant structures such as weapons and war-ware and carriages to battle. Their wives learned to mix of the herbs and their healing properties, and their young men learned the art of handling the sword and to fight with bow and arrow. [1] Daniel 4: 17, 23

35 And it came to pass that Enoch went forth preaching to the people of the land of Saron; of Enoch the son of Cain; of Oener; of Heni; of Sem; of Haner; and the land of Hananiah, settling in the hills and high places to proclaim with a loud voice, words against the works of all men who were offended because of him. And it came to pass that Enoch called all the people unto repentance, with the exception of the people of Cainan; and when they heard him, no man laid his hands upon him; for fear hath taken hold of all that heard his words; and because many began to say that Enoch walked with God, also began to say, that a seer stood up among the people.

36 And so great was his faith, that no sentiment from the dark side could shake his emotional foundations, so that Enoch led the people of God and taught them this same principle, to guard their hearts from any and all adverse sentiments that fall about them, having an unconditional attachment to those feelings which were derived from the greater gift, the Love, through the sentiments that emanated from the names of God, just as he had shown them, when his enemies went out to battle against him and he uttered the word of the Lord, that is, the word that had sprung from their feelings, and the earth trembled, and the mountains crumbled, and the stones rolled, and the rivers turned from their natural courses, the roaring lions roared together in the wilderness; many heard, and trembled.

37 So great was the fear of men that they feared the words spoken by Enoch, for so great was the power of these words that God had given him, through their sentiments and faith, that even the giants, descendants of the sons of God, went away, abandoning their dwellings and the refuge[1] that the watchers[2] had created for them with the help of the earthly man, hiding in caves and deep valleys.

(1) RLDS Genesis 7:18-19 IV / LDS Moses 7:14-15 | **(2)** Daniel 4:17, 23

38 And from that time forth, though there have been wars between men; Enoch knew that Jehovah would come to the temple that Enoch had built for the Lord, because he saw angels descending from heaven, bearing testimony of the Father and the Son[1], and that in the fullness of time He will come to dwell with His people, even as He came to dwell with the people of Enoch before He took them[2], for they shall be as in the days of Enoch, a people who live righteously.

(1) RLDS Genesis 7:33 IV / LDS Moses 7:27 | **(2)** RLDS Genesis 7:20 IV / LDS Moses 7: 16

39 And the fear of the Lord will come upon all nations, for all will see the Lord cross the sky with His entourage of angels and flaming carriages, and as soon as the news will spread throughout every corner, to the farthest reaches of the inhabited earth, that the Lord descended upon His people and entered the thresholds of the temple that will be erected for His name in the last days, in the place that God pre-determined before the foundation of the world, in a Zion that will receive the city of Enoch, whose architecture will design the New Jerusalem.

40 And from that time the Lord blessed the church of Enoch, and called them the people of Zion, because they were all gathered under His laws and commandments, he also blessed the land upon which they had settled, among the mountains, for how much they flourished as a peaceful people, having all the feelings in common.

41 And the Lord called the place of the temple of mount Zion, and their city of Salem, because they were of one heart and purpose, and lived righteously; and there were no poor among them. And so the people of the church of God began to build under the supervision of Enoch a society of holiness, where their citizens would live in their hearts all the principles of purity required by God and be a holy people. They would therefore be a pure people of heart, and called them a covenant people.

42 And it came to pass that Enoch came into the temple before the LORD, and spake face to face with Him, saying: I know, O LORD, that Zion shall dwell in safety for all the time that thou hast with us; but I fear the people shall degenerate after you go, for surely you will not dwell in a temple made by human hands forever, and since we are not a people of wars, as soon as you leave this place, the wicked will attack us. And the Lord answered and said to Enoch: I have indeed blessed the city of Zion, and they shall surely come against you as soon as I depart of this place.

43 And it came to pass that the Lord showed unto Enoch all the inhabitants of the earth; and he looked and saw that Zion was to be caught up and also saw the remnant people that were the sons of Adam; and were a mixture of the whole seed of Adam, among whom many heard the message preached by Enoch and were present in Zion, having in their hearts the same sentiments derived from the name of God as they had the sons of Adam.

44 And after Enoch saw that Zion was taken up into heaven, Enoch looked, and behold, all the nations of the earth stood before him, and Enoch was lifted up and carried away, into the bosom of the Father and of the Son; and behold, he could see the power of Satan and all his influence upon the whole face of the earth. He saw angels descending from heaven to announce the birth of the promised descendant in the meridian of times; and he saw Him also come down in the fullness of time, and later, when he who shall read the words of this sealed book of Moses, arise among the covenant people in the last days and utter with a loud voice the words of God, saying, woe to the inhabitants of the earth, for the day of the Lord is fast approaching, so hear your voice crying out for repentance for the last time.

45 Behold, Enoch saw these days, and Satan had a great chain in his hand, which covered all the face of the earth with darkness; and he looked up and laughed; and his angels mocked over the angels descending from heaven, bearing witness of the Father and the Son; and the Holy Ghost, when He came down upon many, and they were redeemed, by the powers of heaven in Zion.

46 And it came to pass that the God of heaven looked upon the rest of the people, and wept; and Enoch bore witness to this, saying: How canst thou weep, being holy and everlasting for ever and ever? If it were possible for man to count the particles of the earth, yea, of millions of lands like this, it would not even be the beginning of the number of your creations; and the veil of forgetfulness are still stretched; and yet you are merciful and kind to us, the children of man, coming to take Zion to thy own bosom; and mercy shines before your face with tears in your eyes through what I see and your compassion will not end, just as there is no end to your reign. How can you cry?

47 The Lord said to Enoch: "Look at these your brothers; they are the work of My own hands, and I gave them their knowledge in the day that I created them; and in the Garden of Eden I gave man his agency; and I also gave the commandment that they should love one another, and that they should choose Me their Father; but behold, they have no affection for Me, their Creator, and they hate without any reason whatsoever their own kind. How, then, can I, the Lord, show them the kingdoms of other dwellings and the existence of other worlds? Constantly the fire of My indignation is kindled against them; and in My ardent displeasure I will send a flood upon the earth to wash away the filth that man has done against his brother, and to erase forever from the face of the earth his dealings with the children of God and his descendants and the combinations hidden of the order Mahan.

48 Behold, I am the God of Holiness, and I can not tolerate so much filthiness of the flesh before My eyes, where My own angels have entered into a covenant of fornication and adultery with the daughters of men. And although I can extend My arm and hold all My creations; My eyes can not see, among all the works of My hands, as much wickedness as never before existed in between your brethren in all the worlds that I have ever created.

49 But, behold, Satan shall be his father, and the other feelings derived from anguish, which are the fruits of the spirit from the evil one, will be his destiny; which is poured out upon the children of men by their attachment to the sentiments opposed to the true gifts derived from the Holy Spirit of God, and all heaven will weep over them, even all the work of My hands.

50 Therefore, should I not weep, seeing how much they will suffer until they reach the fullness of knowledge that leads them to perfection? — Behold, therefore, I let you know beforehand, that this system which your eyes contemplate will perish in the flood; and behold, I will imprison these disobedient spirits in a prison which I have prepared for them[1], and their cities with their beautiful structures and the corpses of their offspring, I will conceal under the depths of the thickest mud beneath the vast surface layer of earth that covers the ground under his feet[2]. [1] Jude 1:6 | [2] Job 22:15-16

51 For I am bringing upon the earth a new human society, which must begin all over again from the beginning. And as for you and your city, Zion, shall be caught up before arrives this time of calamity which I bring upon the inhabited earth, and I will conceal the old foundations of the sons of God with the coming of the flood except the stone colonnade erected in the center of the city of Zion, and the stones that I will expose from the ancient cities of the Watchers, scattered around the earth, that the children of men after the floods may know that it was from this place that God took the city of Enoch and so that future generations of the sons of men may wonder how the ancients could erect the basis of such complex structures in stones and with perfect precision, even on top of the mountains, and thus be able to conclude by itself, that in ancient times, a race of beings superior to them, yea, the rebellious angels, dominated the world of humanity and enslaved men to serve them, because they allowed themselves that they may be enslaved, and rejected the one who could free them by disobeying My commandments.

52 And now, with the purpose of the people of the covenant to no longer be deceived, when in the last days, yea, before you, Enoch, return with your city to this land, the Watchers who were driven out to the vicinity of Earth, will send signs to the children of men with the promise of ending their diseases, their religions and their false prophets and the scriptures and their false messages and provide them with an alliance, and thus, with the support of satan, the ruler of the world, they will again come to be among you at the invitation of the rulers of the earth, and gradually they will enslave the sons of men again.

53 Except in Zion, where My Only Begotten will have coated His elect of power from on high to overcome the forces of the enemy and to rescue those who are loyal to Me. It is for this reason that I, the Lord, will leave these exposed stones after the flood, so that they may know for themselves that the earthly man has never had the capacity of erecting these old structures, but yea, his dominators.

54 And My Only Begotten begged before My face; therefore, He suffers for the sins of the world, as long as they repent on the day when My Chosen One returns to Me; and until that day they will be in a probation process of constant opposition in all things. For this reason, I, God continually weep for the children of man, and the heavens also weep, yea, and all the work of My hands moan for deliverance, because of the sin of Adam, because he hath brought with him a curse upon the earth and its fruits.

55 And it came to pass that the LORD spake unto Enoch, and told him all the doings of the sons of men; therefore Enoch knew and beheld the iniquities and anguish which came upon them because of the spirit of the evil one; and he wept; and stretched out his arms, and dilated out his heart with eternity; and the bowels were shaken, and all eternity trembled. And Enoch also saw Noah and his family; that the posterity of all the sons of Noah would be saved with a physical salvation. Therefore Enoch saw that Noah built an ark and that the Lord smiled before it and held it in His own hand; but over the rest of the wicked came the floods and swallowed them. Enoch, therefore, wept for his brethren; and said to the heavens, I will refuse to be comforted; but the Lord said to Enoch, "Be blessed and rejoice; and for behold, from Noah, all the families of the earth will wait for My seed[1]." [1] **RLDS Mosiah 8:36-45** | LDS Mosiah 15:9-12

56 And behold, Enoch saw the day of the coming of the Son of Man in the flesh; and his soul rejoiced, saying, Righteousness is lifted up, and the Lamb slain from the foundation of the world; and by faith I will be in the bosom of the Father and behold Zion will be with Me. Enoch, then looked at the Earth; and he heard a voice coming from within, saying: Woe, woe is me, the mother of men; behold I am afflicted, behold I am weary because of the iniquity of my children, and behold, their actions ruin the earth. When will I rest and be cleansed from this filth? When will my Creator sanctify me, that I may rest, and that righteousness remain on my face?

57 This was the lament of the earth, whereby Enoch wept deeply, but the Lord made a covenant with Enoch and swore to him that this vision was interwoven with men at fullness of the times, and the Lord promised Enoch that in these days, He will eliminate those who ruined the earth, and with an oath concerning all His judgments, that would stop the floods after the Flood; and that He should visit the sons of Noah; issuing an unalterable decree that a remnant of his seed would always be found among all nations as long as the earth subsisted; and the Lord said: Blessed is he by whose descendant the chosen seed shall come; for He shall be King over Zion, and shall reign over all the nations of the earth.

58 And it came to pass that Enoch cried unto the LORD, saying: When thy seed come in the flesh, will the earth rest? — And the LORD said unto Enoch: See; and he looked and saw the sign of the Son of Man raised among the men on the earth; and heard a loud voice say; the heavens were covered; and all the works of God wept; and the earth moaned because of their pains[1]; and all the spirits that were in spiritual prisons[2], were visited and received the gospel[3], because the Lord took possession of the key of the spiritual prison and the abyss[4], opening the door for the spirits to enter and bring light and truth to these captives and for others to be freed from the chains of hell, and many went forth, some to judgment of Eternal life[5], and put themselves at the right hand of God; and the others were held in chains of darkness until the judgment of the great day. But behold, Enoch said: Blessed is he by whose offspring shall come the "chosen seed"; and the Lord answering said: I am the descendant Promised, the seed chosen from the foundation of the world, the Messiah, the King of Zion, the Rock of Heaven, and whoever enters by this door shall never fall.[6] [1] Romans 8:20-22 | [2] RLDS Genesis 7:64 - IV; D&C 76:6c-6e; 85:28a-28b / LDS Moses 7:57; D&C 76:73-75; 88:99 | [3] 1Peter 3:18-19; 4:6 | [4] Revelation 1:18; 9:11; 20:1; Luke 16:31 - IV / Luke 16:26 | [5] John 5:25-29 | [6] RLDS Genesis 7:59 - IV / LDS Moses 7: 53

59 And Enoch saw the promised descendant, the Messiah, ascend into heaven; and he cried unto the LORD, saying: You will not return to the earth? — For you are God and I know you; and commanded me to ask in the name of thy Only Begotten; and not by myself, but by your own grace, and I would receive from you what I asked for; therefore, I ask thee whether thou shalt not come again to the earth. And the LORD said unto Enoch: Yea, I the Lord will come in the latter days, in the days of the iniquity of the people, and of the vengeance of God, to fulfill the oath which I did give unto you concerning the sons of Noah; and the day will come when the earth shall rest, but before that day the heavens shall be darkened, and a veil of darkness shall cover the earth; and there shall be great afflictions among the children of men, but My people shall I preserve; and righteousness will I send forth from heaven through My messenger; and I will take from the earth a record of these things, which I reveal to men through My servant, a seer chosen in the opening of the fullness of times, and a second time will be revealed in the final part of the fullness of times, yea, another seer, who will reveal to these sealed words, for the purpose of bearing testimony of the Only Begotten of the Father; of His resurrection from the dead; and also of the resurrection of all men and of the coming of the Only Begotten of the Father among His elect in the last days.

60 It will come after righteousness and truth sweep the earth, before the great and terrifying day of the Lord, when at last I descend upon My people in the last days, just as I came down among you in a temple erected to My name in the land that I will gather My elect, in a place that I will prepare beforehand, a Holy City, so that My people will gird their loins and yearn for the time of My coming; for there will My tabernacle be, and it shall be called Zion, a New Jerusalem[1].

[1] **RLDS 3Nephi 10:3-4; D&C 42:10c** / LDS 3Nephi 21:24-25; D&C 42:35-36

61 And the Lord said to Enoch: Then you will come with all your city and find them there, for your Zion will descend from heaven in this place, and will join you the hundred and forty-four thousand high priests whom I the Lord have ordained according to My holy order, even before the foundation of the world — Priests these, whom God ordained according to the order of His son, and appointed them to be born on earth for the purpose of teaching the covenant people to wait for the promised descendant. Being these, called and ordained to the high priesthood from the foundation of the world, according to the will of God because of the faith they exercised in the plan of redemption from the beginning, when all spirits were in the same position in the spiritual world, before coming to the world, however, these were separated by unconditionally exercising faith in the plan of atonement proposed by the only-begotten Son of the Father. Being therefore, in this way, from the days of Adam until the end of all times, these are those who are born high priests of the holy order of the Son of God in the world of humanity and are ordained by angels[1] to this office, by which they can name other men to the high priesthood of the holy order of the Only Begotten Son of the Father, to teach and administer the commandments of God to the children of men[2]. [1] RLDS - Questions and answers about Book of Revelation / LDS D&C 77:11 | [2] RLDS Alma 9:69 / LDS Alma 13:6

62 Therefore, those who are born high priests among men on earth are seers chosen and ordained by God in the spirit world[1], and are sent when the gospel and its doctrines change, and it is necessary to restore the commandments of God and His church again between the literal descendants of the promise in order to restore the keys of his presidency to their proper place in God's plan in accordance with the eternal course[2]. [1] RLDS Alma 9:62-63 / LDS Alma 13:1 | [2] RLDS D&C 2:1a-2a / LDS D&C 3:1-3

63 And this is the decree established even before the foundation of the world — Every time the gospel goes into apostasy and the keys of the kingdom are spread and lost, behold, God calls a seer. And no man can be the seer, unless he be ordained by God through angels, and become the greatest of all[1], for there can be no greater called among the children of men[2], because the keys are again brought to earth for the purpose of being redistributed to those who will be ordained by his hands to the office of high priests, so to help in matters pertaining to the administration of the church of God, distributing the corresponding keys to all those who hold office of oversight between the covenant people in their respective functions, and who shall be called so that all things pertaining to the kingdom of God occur as organized. **(1)** RLDS D&C 50:6c / LDS D&C 50:26 | **(2)** RLDS Mosiah 5:73-74, 76-77 / LDS Mosiah 8:13, 15-16

64 And it shall come to pass in the last days, that the chosen seed shall be waiting for you, My son Enoch, in the New Jerusalem, and with Him the hundred and forty-four thousand high priests of the holy order of the Son of God, and the people will receive them in their midst and we will embrace; and I will dwell there among the sons of men, fellow citizens of Zion, and for the space of a thousand years the earth shall rest under the rule of My kingdom[1]. **(1)** Revelation 14:1; RLDS D&C 28:2g / LDS D&C 29:11

65 And it came to pass that Enoch saw the day of the coming of the Son of Man in the last days to dwell on the earth in righteousness for the space of a thousand years[1]; but before that day he saw great tribulations among the wicked; and he saw the sea that was shaking, and the hearts of men that were faint, and waited with fear for the judgments of the Almighty God, which were to fall upon the wicked. And the Lord showed Enoch all things, even unto the end of the world; and he saw the day of the righteous, the hour of his redemption; and he received a fullness of joy. **(1)** RLDS D&C 28:2g / LDS D&C 29:11

66 All the days of Zion in the days of Enoch were three hundred and sixty-five years. Enoch and all his people walked with God, and He dwelt in the midst of Zion, as He also promised to dwell among His people in the fullness of time for a thousand years. But, behold, in the last days, as in the days of Enoch, that a building of a spiritual temple should take place before the physical temple is erected among the people of Zion, in which the words of this book will help the people, to carve their hearts hardened by the traditions and precepts of men; to polish their holiness, and to mold them to the true knowledge of My gospel in order to fit like a living stone in the spiritual structure of the temple of God, and after having passed on one generation after another generation, there being no more poor people among them and being of one heart, then there is to be erected a physical temple, where I, the Lord, will descend among My people in the last days, just as it was in the days of Enoch.

67 And, behold, the Zion of Enoch no longer existed, for God received it in His own bosom; and from that time it began to say among the men on earth that Zion was taken away, or that Zion fled.

CHAPTER 5

Methuselah remains on earth to fulfill God's purposes in relation to Enoch's prophecy concerning Noah. Noah preaches repentance to the people but his admonition is ignored. Evil prevails and God decrees destruction of that wicked generation by means of a flood.

1 And all the days of Enoch were four hundred and thirty years. And it came to pass that Methuselah, the son of Enoch, was not taken with Zion, that the covenants which the Lord made with Enoch might be fulfilled in regard to the Priesthood of the Only Begotten in relation to the promised descendant; because He truly made a covenant with Enoch that from the fruit of Noah's loins would come the chosen Seed, promised from the days of Adam.

2 And it came to pass that Methuselah prophesied that out of his loins there were to be born all the kingdoms of the earth through his seed, and, behold, Methuselah lived a hundred and eighty and seven years; and begat Lamech; and Methuselah lived seven hundred and eighty-two years after he begat Lamech, and begat sons and daughters; and all the days of Methuselah were nine hundred and sixty-nine years; and he died.

3 And Lamech lived a hundred and eighty-two years, and begat a son, and named him Noah in reason of the name that was said by

Enoch, and when he saw the newborn child, he perceived that his eyes were different, and he was afraid that Noah would be the son of a watcher[1], but the Spirit of the Lord rested on Lamech, comforting his heart by making him know that he was not a descendant of the watchers, but it was the beginning of a new human progeny. [1] Daniel 4:17, 23

4 Moved, then, by the Holy Spirit, Lamech prophesied, saying, He will comfort us of our toil and in the work of our hands, because of the land which the Lord has cursed. After that Lamech lived five hundred and ninety-five years, and begat sons and daughters; and the days of Lamech were seven hundred seventy and seven years and he died.

5 Noah was four hundred and fifty years old and fathered Japheth; and forty and two years after he begat Shem; and when he was five hundred years old, he begat Ham. For Noah and his sons hearkened unto the LORD, and obeyed His voice; and were called children of God.

6 And God saw that the iniquity of men had become great on the earth; and that all men were arrogant in the thoughts of their heart, being only evil continually. And the Lord said to Noah, Behold, My wrath is kindled against the sons of men, because they do not hearken to My voice; for these wicked men began to multiply on the face of all the earth, and had daughters, and the watchmen who forsook their obedience[1] to Me, the Lord, saw that these daughters were beautiful and were transmuted into the likeness of the sons of men[2], taking them to the wife according to their choices. [1] Jude 1:6 | [2] RLDS Genesis 8:9 - IV / LDS Moses 8:21

7 And it came to pass that Noah prophesied and taught the things of God, as it was in the beginning, saying that for a long time since the very beginning of man's existence, the children of Adam have lived for many years, even as the times of eternity are numbered unto God

— because one day within Eternity is like a thousand years in the kingdom of mankind.

8 Like this, given that God said that if Adam ate the forbidden fruit he would be sentenced to perish on the same day, Adam lived as long as nine hundred and thirty years of age, ending his earthly existence before the end of one day in the time of the Eternity. Thus, all the descendants of Adam inherited this effect on their lives, dying near the thousand year period.

9 However, the Lord said to Noah, My Spirit will not remain in man forever, for he will know that all flesh will die; yet his days shall not be more prolonged in the time period of the heavenly dwelling, but they will be shortened, starting from the flood that I am bringing upon the earth, and if any of the children of Adam give of Me greater pleasure, so I'll make him live longer; and as the dispensations pass, until the coming of My descendant, I will shorten them even more, making them full between seventy and eighty years of age, and some for their robustness, I will permit reach up until one hundred and twenty years old.

10 And, if men will not repent of their sins and will not hearken to the preaching of Noah, then will I send floods upon them, and will I blot out all this iniquity and their cities from the face of the earth, and will create a new lineage of men of the loins of Noah and his seed.

11 And in those days there were giants on earth[1], the descendants of the watcher angels who forsook their natural state to lie with the daughters of men[2]. These, for fear of the words of Noah, which proclaimed destruction upon all them and their offspring, sought Noah to take his life; but the Lord was with Noah and the priesthood power of the Son of God was active in him. And the Lord commanded Noah according to His own command, and commanded that he should declare His gospel to the sons of men, that they should forsake the watchers, and turn away from serving their seed, who were the mighty men of the land; even as it was declared also in the days of Enoch. **(1) RLDS Genesis 8:6 - IV** / LDS Moses 8:18 | **(2) Daniel 4:17, 23; Jude 1:6**

12 And it came to pass that Noah cried unto the children of men that they should repent, but they would not hearken unto his words; and also to the Watchers who had transmuted in the likeness of the sons of men, but when they had heard him, they came before him, saying: Behold, we are the children of God[1]; Have we not taken for ourselves the daughters of men? Are we not eating and drinking and marrying mortal women, just as the sons of Adam do? — And our wives give us children, and they are mighty men like unto your ancestors, yea, the men of old that were among the seed of Adam, as well as Cain and Lamech, who have gained renown among the children of men. **(1) RLDS Genesis 8:9 IV** / LDS Moses 8:21

13 So why should we listen to your cry to leave this Earth and report to God again? — Behold, nothing shall come to us from God, we are His Watchers, it is from us that it is required accountability from this earth, and we will not heed the words of a mere mortal, whose grandfather did not ascend into heaven with the abode of Enoch. And so, out of contempt for Noah and his grandfather Methuselah for they not having gone with the Zion of Enoch, they did not listen to his words, but said that God took Enoch and forsook the remnant of the sons of men to perish in the land.

14 And it came to pass that Noah continued his preaching unto the people of the land, saying: Hearken you, children of Adam, yea, hearken unto my words: believe in what I am proclaiming and repent of your sins and be baptized in the name of the Only Begotten Son of God, as our fathers did before us; and ye shall receive the Holy Spirit[1], that all things may be made manifest unto you; and if you do not, the floods will come upon you. However, they did not listen to his preaching and Noah felt regret and pain in his heart because the Lord had formed man on earth for the purpose of developing spiritually; and it distressed him, because the Lord had said to him that He will make the man which He created on the face of the earth disappear, both man and animals and things that crawl and birds of the air. [1] **RLDS Genesis 6:53; 67-69 - IV / LDS Moses 6:52; 64-66**

15 Noah, for his part, found grace in the sight of the Lord; for he was a just and perfect man in his generation, as was Enoch; and he walked with God, and also his three sons, Shem, Ham, and Japheth.

16 And, behold, God looked upon the earth and it was corrupted before His sight, and God said to Noah, arrived the end of all flesh has for Me, for the earth is full of violence, and the intentions of this human species in its sentiments are only evil all the time, and, behold, I will make all this species, contaminated by the precepts of the order of Mahan and corrupted by watchers angels that abandoned their original position[1] to lie down with the daughters of men, and together with them I will make the ancient cities and their structures disappear once and for all, which were erected by the wisdom of these wicked men, who in ancient times were angels appointed to ride the circuit of heaven, and in the clouds concealed their flaming chariots[2], for the purpose of observing the children of Adam and to present to Me, the Lord, a report of his proceeding with the passing of the ages; but they did not retain their heavenly nature, and were transmuted into the likeness of the children of men as they pleased, for the purpose of bearing offspring which were hybrid to them and distinct from the sons of Adam, surpassing men in size and strength, but dependent on earthly man to elaborate and build according to the appointed designs of their heavenly progenitors, and therefore, the Watchful Angels are now venerated as gods to men on earth as being those who came from the heavens, for the purpose of using the sons of Adam to erect large cities in the service of their offspring. [1] **Jude 1: 6** | [2] **Job 22: 14**

17 For, as I have sworn by Myself, I will sever the bond with those wicked men who did not retain their celestial origin, before the time predetermined by Me, the Lord, so that they may be judged and condemned by Gabriel the upper sentinel of the order of the star D'alva, which commands the seraphs with their chariots of fire and the vigilantes who introduce themselves and mingle among men on earth to ascertain the facts between them, often coexisting in its environment[1], in order to make a report of the kingdom of mankind and to present from time to time in front of the great council of the heavens[2]. [1] Book of Tobit 5:1-20 | [2] Hebrews 12: 22-24

18 For how much I, the Lord, will pour out upon all these cities, erected in the likeness of the things that are in the abode of the heavens, a flood to hide under the mire, all their foundations[1], that mankind may never discover the systems of their societies elaborated by the wisdom of some watchmen who did not obey the original command from Me, the Lord[2]. [1] Job 22: 16 | [2] Jude 1:6

19 For, behold, after the flood I, the Lord, will renew all things and Noah and his descendants will build a new society upon old structures, and I will cause them to forget these things hidden under their feet. Then when the sons of men multiply again on the face of the earth, I will build them up in the land which I have appointed them, and they shall be no more removed from the land which I have given them. And I will certainly repair the hearts of the children of Adam, and I will erect in the final part of all time a holy people upon the world of mankind, as I have always desired.

20 And then the flood came and swept them all except Noah and his family by whose hand God preserved a righteous offspring of the children of Adam to recommence everything anew, and through him preserved all the animals that the Lord selected.

21 This, therefore, is briefly the story of Noah, because the rest was written by me, Moses, in another record, so that people will know at the time when this book sealed is revealed, that God has indeed appointed a great flood to come upon all the earth and its confines, in order to destroy the structures formerly left behind by the ancient kings from the loins of Azaziel and his confederated watchmen who came of the skies and subdued the sons of men to build cities and kingdoms without the consent of God, because they reigned over men in such a length of time that it becomes improper to mention, although some of its foundations, those which were erected above on the top of the mountains, were not all completely destroyed by the waters of the flood, as it was shown to me in a vision, when I, Moses, saw in one instant all things concerning this world.

22 Therefore, I begin again to tell the history of the world of mankind in a summarized way, so that all the children of men understand in their hearts and transmit poetically the history of their origins, from generation to generation for their descendants. For I alone, Moses, will know the truth of all things concerning the dealings of God, from beginning to end, as it has been shown unto me, but they shall not come to the knowledge of men, until they are ready to understand them; of some generations, after the knowledge of this book is revealed to those who believe, whose children will be taught rightly about its precepts.

23 I, Moses, speak this way, because in truth, yea, in the fullest truth that this fact can be told, I say to them, when in the fullness of times comes the time to be opened the knowledge of this book to men in the flesh, that I, Moses write and then I will seal, for a wise purpose in the future; but behold the men of this generation will not be fully ready to understand the truths here exposed, except to those who seek the mysteries of God in their hearts.

24 There shall be among them a Moses like unto me, who shall bring forth the words of this book, and of others which shall be jointly sealed to this, to complement the essence of the truth which hath been hidden in the midst of the scriptures of prophets of God which formerly lived on this earth, and to this Moses, who shall read the words of this book, he shall be given understanding of all things concerning knowledge hidden in these words which were left unto me by God.

25 And he will be the instructor of those who will lay the foundations of a new society among the children of men, by whose fruits of the Spirit of God, the heavenly gifts that subsist in their hearts, may by their guidance be fully developed among the people of the Lord in the last days, just as I, Moses, had the opportunity to work such gifts on the children of Israel when they left Egypt, and after having used in their fullness the power from these gifts, either by the grace of God which was poured out abundantly upon those who did not possess the holy priesthood of the Only Begotten Son, but for their faith in His name, as regards men and women who were baptized under the cloud, meaning that they were in a condition covenanted with Jehovah, just as their manifestations also took place among the Priests of their sacred Order, the likeness of the Only Begotten of the Father.

26 To these I, Moses, clearly taught them in the wilderness and diligently sought to sanctify the nation of Israel in their totality, purifying their hearts so that their feelings would be the purest possible, in order to take upon themselves the name of God and to the Grace and power of the priesthood among their descendants and thus be able to get and to live in its fullness the law of consecration for the purpose of becoming equal to the people of Enoch, in one a perfect, united order.

27 For behold, verily I say unto you, that the gifts of God are but the pure sentiments derived from His name in their hearts, and for being so simple to the class of the sages of Israel, such gifts did not subsist for long in their midst, for how much they were not able to bear His presence in their feelings, but as soon as they hardened their hearts because of the precepts which they had in regard to their traditions, that it was not possible to pass on this knowledge to their children and to these future generations, but only one among so many men of the house of Israel was able to understand, yea, Joshua.

28 Not even my children were able to comprehend the fullness of these things, due to the precepts passed to them by my father-in-law Jethro. Because the Lord has demanded of me, Moses, that after I have written these words, that I may be taken out of this people, Israel, and from among them, even the priesthood of His Son be taken away, lest they belittle this greater gift; the love coming from the higher name of God and thus they come to desecrate its meaning. Therefore it must remain hidden from the world until this book is revealed in the fullness of times, but not all will understand except those who believe.

29 Therefore, I, Moses, tell you again this truth, that the children of men who shall receive these things, when in the fullness of time comes, that they will not yet be fully ready to comprehend in its fullness the truths here exposed, except to those who seek to understand the mysteries of God.

30 This will naturally occur, not because of excessive attachment to their traditions, because the things here written by me, Moses, under the influence of the Holy Spirit, will be as clear and precious as the purest and crystalline water to drink in a thirsty desert; a clear source in regard to everything else that will already be contaminated and polluted by the precepts of men.

31 It will then be given, according to the things written by the prophets that here on this earth and beyond the great waters will live, but that they will never perceive the hidden truth behind the previous writings. Coming to know, that the Gifts derived from the Fruits of the Holy Spirit are in fact pure feelings coming from a sanctified heart, in whose Greatest Gift, love, hides the fullness of God's power.

32 This Gift to be used by grace, temporarily allowed to one who attains divine recognition by means of supplication and prayer, or by means of an authorized representative of the Son of the Only Begotten of the Father in the flesh, by whose priestly office He allows him to use that greater feeling, or even of other derivatives of it, that if allows to flow, and that frees; that awakens; that is reborn; that renews and, finally, that sculpts the human character, and dignifies him according to the divine personality, in a higher being, coated of charity and compassion.

33 I'm not talking about pity, because to pity someone, is a petty feeling derived from the evil one. But above all, I am talking about empathy, when we want others to have the greater good that we have or want to have.

34 Therefore, guard your heart from the feelings derived from worldly passions and desires, for all these come from the influence of evil. Ensure that your soul is not affected by feelings of fear and doubt, for these are contrary to the courage to which we have been clothed in the spirit even before the foundation of the world and the faith we should have in connection with God the Father, and that we can know in the fullness of our being that the solution of all adversities that stand in the way against our existence here on this earth rests, not on our human capacity and fallen, but in God, who can do everything, and for whom there is no impossibility.

35 For how much a sincere prayer, made with a broken heart and a contrite spirit, is enough to move the hand of Him who commands the whole universe.

36 Nevertheless, many in this generation will have the desire to practice these truths when they read the words of this book, but they will be impregnated with the evil feelings in their way of feeling, which from the beginning has been taught by the parents to inhibit their gifts, without any of them realizing that it is infecting the feelings of their offspring with the gifts coming from the Mahan Order.

37 Which will make it almost impossible to experience in their fullness the purity of the gifts of the Holy Spirit in their hearts, as far as this generation is concerned - for they will, on occasion, return to a petty feeling that is part of their personality, of their traditions, of their customs, and of their prejudices, for how much, one tries to experience the good feelings described here, however little understood by this generation.

38 Therefore, even though they fully understand these words of mine in relation to the gifts of the Spirit; nevertheless, it will be a constant struggle to guard against the influence of the evil one, and with that, not be overwhelmed by feelings of fear, anger, envy, pride, greed and other derivatives of the iniquity.

39 Only by having purity of heart can feelings of holiness be attained, for this is to be holy, to be pure before God. And only with a pure heart and united in the sentiments derived from the name of the Most High; taking upon himself the name of His Only Begotten Son, is that the people will become Zion in the last days, just as Enoch exalted the feelings of his people before the Flood swept the earth and they were caught up in their days.

40 So this book will not suddenly change the generation of those who will obtain it firsthand, but before rather it will be preached to all nations upon instruction from this one, a Moses like me, and after this generation, their children and the children of their children will be full of holiness, and the gifts derived from the Holy Spirit will be natural in their way of feeling; inhibiting the power and influence of the enemy wherever they preach this good news of the Kingdom.

41 Thereafter, Zion will coexist among the children of men, beginning in the hearts of the people of the church of the Lamb of God in the last days, which will be taken out of obscurity and darkness, when then the words of this book are given to read for those who believe, for they will be able to build their structures before abandoned by pride and other sentiments derived from the evil one who sat among the priests of the Most High in the fullness of times.

42 And after the church of the Lamb is again structured, having as a foundation the pillars of protection of the truth, as stipulated in the everlasting and unchanging gospel of the Father, from the beginning to the end of all times[1], behold, the words of this book shall be preached to all nations, for the benefit of the children of Adam to those who believe in his words and are baptized in the name of the Only Begotten of the Father. **(1)** RLDS Genesis 6:7 IV / LDS Moses 6:7

CHAPTER 6

This is the story of Nimrod son of Cush; who was the son of Ham; who was Noah's son - the first man to become mighty on earth after the days of the Flood. He became a mighty hunter in opposition to Jehovah.

1 Before the Flood, there was water on the surrounding layer of the sky, for on the second day of creation, God made an expansion around the earth, and upon this expansion there was indeed a separation between the waters beneath it, that is, the oceans, and the waters above it — for from ancient times there was a surface of water in the sky, shimmering in the light of the sun, which covered the whole surface of the earth. Because of this there were fruits and seeds in abundance everywhere, for behold, a dew rose from the ground every day, and watered all the plants and there were no deserts, but all the land was productive.
2 Nevertheless, after the Flood occurred, behold, the whole surface of the earth underwent a drastic change, for behold, all the springs of the vast water of depth were broken, and the floodgates of the heavens were opened, and even the lofty hills were covered, all that were under all the heavens.

3 As soon as the waters of the Flood descended, behold, God commanded Noah to awaken all the animals one last time, because God had made them sleep according to the time it was necessary to sleep for a long period of time, until he woke them up, for the third and last time, slowly, one at a time, so that from there they would spread to the ends of the earth and spread the seeds they carried within themselves, to germinate the earth again; quadruped animals; and beasts; and reptiles of the earth; and birds of the sky; Yea, everyone, no matter the species, from small to great, all the animals that had hitherto been fed on all kinds of seeds and fruit, since God had decreed to the descendants of Noah the command to feed on all that moves on the face of the earth and also for the animals not to die of hunger, since the earth would no longer deliver its fruit in abundance as it happened before the Deluge.

4 And so, as before God gave us the vegetables and their seeds, now God was saying that all living things can be food for both men and animals, for there was nothing on the surface of the ground to feed them. And God blessed all living beings, that they might be fruitful, and replenish the earth, every man according to his kind.

5 It was then given that after releasing the beasts, that God commanded Noah to gather and sprinkle on the flat roof of the ark, all the seeds which he had stocked upon the command of God, to be planted again after the Flood, and, behold that a wind from the north blew above the ark, and the seeds were scattered about where Noah and his family were, and to the four corners of the earth; and wherever they fell, they quickly germinated and bore fruit according to their kind.

6 Among the sons of Noah were the descendants of Japheth; Tarshish, Kittim, and Dodanim, who began to use the knowledge of Japheth in the building of the ark to build great fishing vessels, and from these came the first inhabitants of the islands that spread themselves over their territories, and though they all spoke the same language, every new place inhabited, developed their own customs of speech, according to their families and according to their nations.

7 Then, after the Flood and the destruction of all the ungodly people in the world of mankind, Noah and his descendants were to rebuild the new earth, which would be pure in the sight of God, for all the earth had passed away by a baptism, for the purpose of representing a new creation in the sight of the heavens.

8 It was thus that true worship was restored again by Noah and the other seven survivors of the Flood at the beginning of the time they left the ark as a symbol of deliverance for offering sacrifices to Jehovah under Noah's leadership, he built an altar to God and took some of all the pure animals and all the pure flying creatures that were among them, and made burnt offerings on the altar in praise and thanks to God for His act of salvation in regard to the sons of men and all the animals He selected to exist on the inhabited earth.

9 But the adversary of God, Satan, the devil, was still lurking in order to distill his spirit in the sons of Noah, as he had in the beginning with the descendants of Adam and Eve. And it came to pass, that Satan found in the young Nimrod, the son of Cush, descending from Ham, the same rebellious disposition that he had found in Cain for his ancestor Noah.

10 After Nimrod heard from his father the account in which his grandfather discovered the nakedness of Noah, and that he became drunk, behold, this caused him repugnance for his grandfather.

11 Satan, therefore, begins to interact in his sentiments, and to develop in Nimrod, for how much he was still a boy, the desire to overlap the blessing of Noah upon his descendant Shem, that it would be through him and his seed that the future descendant would come, through the genealogy of the righteous descendants of Adam, to Abram, whom God later took from among the people of Ur of the Chaldees, to strengthen their covenant with the righteous sons of Adam, to begin with Seth; Enos; Cainan; Mahalaleel; Jared; Enoch;

Methuselah; Lamech; Noah; Shem; Arphaxad; Salah; Eber; Peleg; Reu; Serug; Nahor; Terah and Abram. — Therefore, Nimrod would be outside the presidency of the priesthood, and even of possibility of the promised descendant coming from his seed.

12 It was then that Satan proceeded to stir up the heart of Nimrod for the purpose of becoming a mighty hunter in opposition to Jehovah, which means in the language of the Hebrews – "hunter of men", that is, one who hunts men with purpose of enslaving, thus acting in opposition to the precepts of freedom extended to all men created by Jehovah. — In this way, Nimrod, backed by Satan, became a warrior and conqueror of people.

CHAPTER 7

Nimrod himself elects the promised descendant, babel is built, builds cities; creates schools of wisdom for the purpose of nullifying the gift of God in children.

1 After the Flood, all the land was still of the same language and dialect and parents had the custom to teach their children about the good feelings from the Spirit of God, in such a way, that such teaching became natural after the flood among the descendants of Noah, as God had designed.

2 But it came to pass that one of the descendants of Ham, under the influence of Satan, sought in his heart to have full control over the children of men, entering into the towns and villages, killing men and taking captive children and women, and enslaving all those who did not agree with his command.

3 To those who were subject to his power, these were commissioned to act in their many duties, whether in the planting and harvesting of fruits and cereals; in the management of cattle and animals of slaughter, in the creation of bricks and construction of houses and protective walls; in the production of weapons and ornaments of wars, and the most robust and active were commissioned to be in the military service, because they settled in a valley in the land of Shinar.

4 And with the growth of the people around him, Nimrod proceeded to select chiefs who responded by him to the people, and they said to one another: "let's make brick and cook it well with fire". And they said: "Let the people of Shinar come, let us build ourselves a city and a tower whose summit shall rise up very near the heaven where we may establish a door for the 'promised descendant' to enter the dwelling of God; and let us make a name for ourselves, that we may not be scattered throughout the face of the whole earth, but be remembered by generation after generation, why the fated seed is with us, even Nimrod, the mighty among the children of men."

5 With the propagation of the word that the promised descendant was in the world, and was ruler in his own kingdom, many other people deliberately began to join him on the plain of Shinar, for how much it was necessary to erect more cities to accommodate the population, all around the land of his government, some more distant than others by reason of the ore and other artifacts that added value to his reign, and thus, Nimrod also began to call kings, to govern these cities, but they were only vassals of his kingdom and subjects to his command.

6 The men at that time knew very well that God had made a promise to His descendant, but no one knew how and when His descendant would come to reign among the sons of Adam. With this, Satan began to twist the meaning of the promise and apply it to Nimrod, who came to take advantage of this circumstance, since from his youth he sought in his heart to obtain the presidency of the Priesthood of the Only Begotten Son of God, and now, he found himself at the head of the Priesthood presidency, in the royal position of the promised descendant.

7 In harmony with their selfish desire to create for themselves a great name, he elected himself, as the promised descendant. It was then that Nimrod chose a priestly caste to represent him as the son of God. — These priests, in turn, came to obtain help from Satan, by means of powerful works and portents, little by little, began to create hierarchies and priestly garments; and by means of signs and handshakes, began to separate the high priests from those who were less important.

8 Soon, the high priests of the order Mahan began to form dogmas in relation to the promised descendant and to reverse the correct pronunciation of the name Nimrod for the pronouncing Marduk which means "the Lord."

9 In these days, when Nimrod succeeded in promoting false self-worship as the promised descendant, he and his confederates began spreading the priestcraft through the land to keep the absolute control of the children of men, and being known this secret only the priestly caste in which he is "the Lord" of this great secret and high priest of the Mahan order, therefore Marduk.

10 He knew that the gifts of the Spirit of God were pure and elevated feelings and that they had been passed on from father to son since the days of Noah. He also knew that such feelings, united with the priesthood of the Son of God, whose keys rested on Shem and his offspring, and active in the descendants of Japheth, would soon obstruct the spread of his reign beyond the land of Shinar.

11 With this he proposed that a school of wisdom should be instituted in the cities he built, where children of all peoples of the earth would receive instruction at the highest level, improving their knowledge in the writing; in astrology; mathematics, architecture; construction; music and religion.

12 This would all be offered free to all peoples, where children would enjoy the best accommodations and food Nimrod had to offer. — With this was drawn up a decree that was taken by his messengers to the four corners of the earth, where there was a family residing, this family should then be informed of the benevolence of Nimrod.

13 The purpose, though it seemed noble, was clothed with priestcraft through; of illusion and obscurity — the master-priests who were being prepared to teach the children brought by their fathers to this supposed school of wisdom had as their guideline the nullifying of the gifts of the Spirit of God in their hearts, making them believe in the opposite of everything they had been taught by their parents before entering what the high priesthood of Marduk called among the children of men, as being the doors of wisdom.

14 The instructions were clear, everything in that children believe, infallibly would be attributed to the power of evil, so if one were to see their father use the gift of the Spirit to heal someone in his family, or even to obtain miraculous help from the heavens, they would immediately rebuke their father and mother of such proceeding, claiming that they themselves were deceived in the beginning when their ancestors used magic and witchcraft to gain benefit from the spiritual world.

15 This mode of teaching was widely accepted among the peoples of the earth, and in a short time the power and influence of the gifts from the Spirit of God ceased to exist in their fullness in the feelings of men, and once again their hearts were contaminated by precepts of men and poisoned by the spirit of Satan.

16 Many of these children underwent the priestly initiation of the school of Marduk, in order to perpetuate the subservience of the children of men to a man in the office of God. And when God spread the people to the four corners of the earth, it was these young priestly apprentices who later founded kingdoms with the same principle, where a man was venerated as the son of God, or of the gods, because there was a mixture of doctrines between the people that were gathered together in the land of Shinar.

CHAPTER 8

The Lord descends to see what is happening; He sees the construction of the tower of babel; God confounds the language of the peoples, Abram arises.

1 And the LORD came down, and saw the city, and the tower, which the children of men were building; and the Lord said, Behold, the people are one, and they all have one tongue; and for this reason they began to build this tower, because they look at the words of a single man who is promoted in the position of a god among the men in the flesh. And now there will be no restriction on what they intend to do, unless I, the Lord, confuse their language, so that no one understands the pronunciation of each other. For I the Lord, I will scatter them on the face of the earth, between the four corners of the world.

2 Then it came to pass that the men no longer understood one another, and this caused strife and great confusion among them, and because they no longer understood the commands of their kings and lords, they stopped building the city and began, each seeking those who spoke a language understandable to oneself, in order to depart from that place which they started to call themselves 'confusion'.

3 And therefore it is called Babel, because the Lord was displeased with their works, and it was at that time in the history of the earthly man, that the Lord confounded and mixed the tongue of every man, woman, and child of that place; and from there the Lord scattered them on every corner of the earth.

4 And these were the generations of Shem the son of Noah, the high priest of the holy order of the priesthood of the Son of God, who begot Arphaxad at the age of a hundred years, only two years after the flood. And Shem did live five hundred years, and begat sons and daughters. Arphaxad lived thirty-five years, and begat Salah; and Arphaxad lived after he begat Salah four hundred and three years; and begat sons and daughters. And Salah lived thirty years, and begat Eber; and after he begat Eber, he lived four hundred and three years, and begat sons and daughters. Eber lived thirty-four years, and begot Peleg; and Eber lived after he begat Peleg four hundred and thirty years, and begat sons and daughters. Peleg lived thirty years and begot Reu; and lived after he had begotten Reu, two hundred and nine years, and begot sons and daughters. Reu lived thirty-two years and begot Serug; and Reu lived after he begat Serug, two hundred and seven years, and begat sons and daughters. Serug lived thirty years and begot Nahor; and Serug lived after he begat Nahor two hundred years, and begat sons and daughters. Nahor lived twenty-nine years and begot Terah; Nahor lived after he begat Terah, a hundred and nineteen years, and begat sons and daughters. And Terah lived seventy years, and begat Abram, Nahor, and Haran.

5 These were the generations of Terah; when he begat Abram, Nahor, and Haran; and Haran became the father of Lot. But Haran died before his father Terah, in the land of his birth, in Ur of the Chaldees.

6 Abram and Nahor took for themselves wives; and the name of the wife of Abram was Sarai, and the name of Nahor's wife Milcah the daughter of Haran, the father of Milcah and Isca. But Sarai was barren and had no son. In these days Terah took Abram his son, and Lot, son of Haran, son of his son, and Sarai his daughter-in-law, wife of his son Abram, and he went out with them from Ur of the Chaldees to go to Canaan; and they dwelt there.

CHAPTER 9

Abram shares the sacrament with his family, pays tithes to Melchizedek; the priesthood is active in Abram; Melchizedek blesses Abram.

1 When he returned from the battle, he gave the tithe of all war spoils to Melchizedek, as well as all that he possessed, showing that even he, who would become the father of our faith, was not exempt from the law of tithing. Then Melchizedek, king of Salem, and high priest of the Most High God, took bread and wine[1]; and laid it on the altar, and blessed the bread, and brake it[2], and gave Abram first to eat, whom he had appointed to the priesthood, by whose priestly power proceeding from the name of the Father, and of the Son, and of the Holy Spirit, was active in him in the midst of the battle of Chedorlaomer. [1] Acts of Three Nephites 2:1 | [2] RLDS Genesis 14:17-18 - IV

2 And he also shared the bread and wine with the family of Abram, and with all his servants that were under the covenant. So Melchizedek proceeded, symbolically in relation with the promise made since the days of Adam, of the promised descendant who is King and Priest of the Most High forever in the manner of Melchizedek.

3 For how much, the other confederate kings who were in battle, were only permitted to watch this sacred ceremony with their ordinances. And after Melchizedek had distributed the sacrament, being the high priest of the Most High God, called Abram and blessed him, saying: Blessed be Abram, thou art the man of the Most High God, possessor of the heavens and the earth, and blessed be the Most High God, who delivered his enemies into his hands.

4 And after washing his feet in a ceremony to show him that the greatness of the greater is to serve as a minor, he confirmed him to the office of High Priest, saying: Blessed be Abram, a man of faith; receives, therefore, this consecration[1] and called to direct the church that will henceforth be known by the name of the Most High through its descendants until it is put on the head of another[2] by oath and covenant[3], from the beginning to the end of times[4]. [1] Acts of Three Nephites 2:2; RLDS Alma 3:3 /Alma LDS 5:3 | [2] RLDS D&C 83:6d-6e / LDS D&C 84:34-36 | [3] RLDS D&C 83:6f-6g / LDS D&C 84:39-40 | [4] RLDS Genesis 6:7 - IV / LDS Moses 6:7

5 And it came to pass before all the kings of the earth that Melchizedek raised his voice and blessed Abram, confirming him to the high priesthood of the holy order of the Only Begotten of the Father. — Being this Melchizedek recognized by all of them; for before he obtained the scepter of the king, he was a man of faith, who did righteousness among his people; and when he was a boy, he covered the mouths of lions, and extinguished the fiery impetuous that consumed his village by the tyranny of the vassals of Nimrod.

6 And so, being approved of God, he was ordained a high priest according to the order of the covenant which God made with Enoch, which was according to the order of the Son of God; whose existence does not come from the earthly man, nor from the will of man; neither by father nor mother; nor by the beginning of days nor by the end of years; but of God; whose Son proposed in Himself, before the foundation of the world, to gather together all things, both things in the heavens and on earth, which were being extended to the children of men by the appeal of His own voice, through His prophets according to His will, to all who believe and yet will believe in His name.

7 For God swore to Enoch and his descendants with an oath unto Himself; that all who are ordained according to this command and call, would have power by faith, to divide the seas, to dry the waters, to divert the course of the rivers, and to move the mountains from their place. In defying so many natural elements as the armies of nations, to divide the earth, to break all ties of the enemy, and to stand in the presence of God; simply by doing all things according to His will, according to His commandments, and even to subdue against principalities and powers; if so the will of the Son of God that existed before the foundation of the world. Therefore, in the days of Enoch this Priesthood was called by his name, as being the priesthood of Enoch[1]. [1] **RLDS D&C 76:5g** / LDS D&C 76:57

8 And the men who had this faith before the foundation of the world were ordained by this holy calling, in the order of God, in the likeness of Melchizedek, who was also high priest of the same order as Enoch before him, but as Melchizedek was greater than Enoch in the likeness of the Only Begotten of the Father; having been called and prepared from the foundation of the world, according to the will of God who called and ordained him, first by His foreknowledge and then according to his great faith, for the purpose of teaching the commandments of God to the children of men[1], was that the Priesthood of the Son of God in relation to the great high priest which was Melchizedek, and out of respect or reverence to the name of the Supreme Being and, so that men not abuse the gifts derived from the feelings that come from the name of God, came to be called according to the order of Melchizedek[2]. [1] **RLDS Alma 9:62-71; 10:7** / LDS Alma 13:1-7, 14 | [2] **RLDS D&C 104:1c** / LDS D&C 107:4

9 And when there is on earth a high priest appointed by the heavens in the manner of Melchizedek, for the purpose of regulating the gospel of the Lamb of God, which in some way has become distorted among the children of men; he must be caught up to receive the keys of the same high priesthood in his body[1], as a slave marked by his Lord, as if it were, by an incandescent iron, both physically and spiritually, and therefore Melchizedek was called the Prince of Peace, because he had the power to unify the people of God, just as he unified Abram under the covenant and conferred upon him the presidency of this high priesthood and blessed Abram with all gifts pertinent to the president of the church[2] among the people of God in their days. But Melchizedek remained the greatest, though he was minor among them, for how much he lived[3]. [1] Galatians 6:17 | [2] RLDS D&C 104:31e / LDS D&C 107:64-67 | [3] RLDS D&C 104:42a-42b / LDS D&C 107:91-92

10 For behold, Abram made all things by revelation received from heaven, and obtained from the Lord the promise that his righteous offspring would forever inherit this same priesthood from the holy order of the Son of God; and that God will raise a prophet the likeness of Melchizedek, from times to times, to bring light and knowledge to the children of men in the flesh, for the purpose of uniting the heavens and the earth, when in the final part of all times the city of Enoch will descend again to the church of the lamb. But the children of God shall be tested by fire.

11 And this Melchizedek, having established righteousness on earth, was called the king of the heavens by his people, or, in other words, the King of peace. Because he lifted up his voice, and blessed Abram, being the high priest and keeper of the Lord's storehouse, the one that God appointed to receive tithes for the poor. So even Abram paid him the tithes of all that he had, which God gave him, which exceeded his needs.

12 And it came to pass that God blessed Abraham, and gave him riches and glory, and lands for an everlasting possession; according to the covenant he made, and according to the blessing which Melchizedek had blessed him.

CHAPTER 10

God establishes a covenant with Abram and his descendants.

1 It was then, that it obscured the time in which the Lord God if showed, in the understanding of Abram, with the irrevocable promise to obtain the earth for an eternal inheritance. And Abram said: Lord God, how wilt thou give me this land for an eternal inheritance, if I die?

2 And, behold, the Lord said: Though you are dead, could not the Lord give you your inheritance? — And if you die, yet you shall still possess this good land, for verily I say unto you, the hour is come that the Son of Man shall rise again to obtain eternal life. But how could he revive, if he were not dead? Does he not at first have to be vivified?

3 And it came to pass that Abram looked on and saw the days of the Son of Man, and rejoiced as he became acquainted with the Resurrection and the mortal ministry of the Only Begotten of the Father in the meridian of times; and his soul found rest in this vision, and he believed in the Lord; and the Lord conceived this as being justice and righteousness.

4 And it came to pass that Abram fell to the ground, and called on the name of the LORD in his heart; and God continued to speak with him, saying: My people have departed from My precepts, and have not kept My judgments which I gave to their fathers; they did not observe My anointing nor the burial or baptism which I commanded them; but they turned aside from the commandment, and took to themselves the washing of little children, and the blood of the sprinkling; and they affirm that the blood of righteous Abel was shed for sins; and do not understand that they are all responsible for their acts before Me, the Lord.

5 But as for you, Abram, behold, I will make My covenant with thee, and thou shalt be the father of many nations. And this covenant I do that your children may be known among all nations. And you shall no more be called Abram, but thy name shall be Abraham; for I will make thee a father of many nations, and I will make thee fruitful and nations shall come out of thy seed, and kings shall come forth out of thy lineage; and of thy priesthood[1]. [(1)] **RLDS 1Nephi 4:28-29** / LDS 1Nephi 15:18

6 Behold, I, the Lord, establish with thee a covenant of circumcision. And it shall be a covenant between Me and thee, and thy seed after thee, for all the generations of the earth. However, children are not responsible before My eyes until they are eight years old; but after being in the age of knowledge, behold, thou shalt seek to teach thy children to keep all My covenants, to begin with the baptism which I have commanded them; by which I the Lord have made covenant with thy ancestors in the priesthood of My Only Begotten; and keep the commandments which I gave thee by My own mouth; and I will be God to you and to your seed after you, who shall keep these My commandments and be a representative of My name among the sons of men and a blessing to all nations — Amen.

CHAPTER 11

Israel's patriarchal blessing on Judah and Joseph, and his sons, Manasseh and Ephraim.

1 Judah, your brothers will praise you; Your hand will be on the neck of your enemies and the sons of your father shall bow down before your seed. For how much it is still a lion's cub, it is not the time of Judah to eat prey. Bow down for a while, my son, and lay down upon the nations of the earth like an adult lion roaring. — "Who among men will dare to awaken him?"

2 The scepter shall not depart from Judah, nor the lawgiver from between his feet, until Shiloh comes, the promised descendant; and the peoples of the earth shall be gathered unto Him for all generations of Israel, to rise again in the fullness of all times, as King over all nations.

3 And Jacob laid his hands upon the head of Joseph, and said: When the God of my fathers appeared to me at Luz in the land of Canaan, He swore to me that He would give me and my seed the land for a perpetual possession. Behold, therefore, O my son Joseph, God hath blessed me, taking you far from me, to save the house of Israel, His servant, from death; in delivering my people and thy brethren from the famine that was grievous in the land.

4 Therefore, the God of thy fathers shall bless thee, and the fruit of thy loins, that they may be blessed above thy brethren, and above the house of thy father; for thou hast prevailed, and thy father's house has bowed down before thee, as it was shown thee in a dream, before you were sold to the Egypt by the hands of thy brethren; therefore, your brethren shall bow down to you from generation to generation, to the fruit of your loins forever.

5 And behold, thou shalt be a light unto my people in the last days, to deliver them in the days of their captivity, from bondage to the precepts of men; and to bring them salvation, when they are completely bowed down under the sin of obstinacy in their hearts.

6 You are, therefore, a fruitful branch together with the source of My power, coming from My priesthood; and its branches run about the wall that separates the lands beyond the sea. For how much the archers of death will give him bitterness, because they hate him without cause, but his bow will stand firm, and the arms of his offspring, they will be stretching the ropes of this last dart, coming from your bag of arrows, and will be strengthened by the hands of the valiant of Jacob, from where the shepherd and the stone of Israel come.

7 By the God of your father and by the Almighty, who will bless you with blessings from above; for how much the blessings of thy father have prevailed above the blessings of my progenitors unto the utmost bound of the everlasting hills; they shall be on the head of

Joseph, and on the head of Ephraim, who was separated by the Lord off from among his brethren.

8 And now upon thy two sons, Ephraim and Manasseh, who were born to thee in the land of Egypt, before I came to thee in this foreign land, behold, just as Reuben and Simeon will be blessed, for they are mine; then thy children shall be called after my name, for they are of the house of Israel.

9 But, behold, your offspring, which you shall bear after them, shall be yours; and they shall be called after the name of their brethren in their inheritance, in the tribes that shall come from their loins; therefore they shall be called, as the tribes of Manasseh and Ephraim.

CHAPTER 12

Joseph prophesies in Egypt that Moses will deliver Israel from the Egyptian captivity; God reveals to Joseph that a branch of his descendants will be taken to a distant land, and from his loins two seers and a mouthpiece will come to the aid of a Moses whom the Lord will raise up in the last days.

1 And Joseph said unto his brethren: The Lord hath visited me, and I have obtained a promise from Him, that the Lord God shall raise up a just branch from the loins of Jacob, a prophet; not the promised descendant. And behold, this prophet shall deliver my people out in the days of their bondage.

2 And it shall come to pass that they shall be scattered again; and a branch shall be broken, and brought to a far country, beyond the sea; nevertheless, they shall be remembered in the covenants of the Lord, when the Messiah shall come; for it will be revealed to them in the last days, in the Spirit of power; and he shall bring them out of darkness into the light; from hidden darkness, and from captivity to eternal freedom. And a seer, God will lift from the fruit of my loins, who shall be a seer chosen to restore the ordinances of the house of Israel in this far land.

3 And the God of my fathers said unto me: Joseph, a chosen seer will I raise up out of the fruit of thy loins, and he shall be highly esteemed; and I will command him to do a work for the fruit of thy loins: for whosoever shall accept his words, and be baptized because of them, shall be numbered as part of the house of Ephraim, whom I have separated among his brothers. Therefore, a descendant of Joseph, the brother of Manasseh, to whom he shall be taken first to this place far beyond the great waters; and they shall be a remnant branch of the house of Jacob. And he will bring you to know the covenants which I made with your fathers; and he shall perform whatever work I command him.

4 And, lo, I, the Lord, will make him great; and he shall be in My sight like Moses, and his name shall be known among all nations, for he shall do My work. Yea, truly he will be like Moses, which I said that I would raise up to deliver My people, O house of Israel, from the oppression like the slaves; for behold, I will raise up a seer to deliver My people out of the land of Egypt; and he shall be called by the name of Moses. And by that name his brethren shall know that he belongeth unto the house of Israel.

5 Therefore, the fruit of thy loins shall write a record as soon as his offspring obtain this land beyond the sea; and the fruit of the loins of Judah shall also write a record; and that which is written by the fruit of thy loins in this far country, and that which is written by the fruit of the loins of Judah, shall grow together, each in his own nation, for the purpose of confounding false doctrines, and appeasing contentions, and establishing peace between the fruit of thy loins and the house of Jacob in the last days; when then, the words of these two records are brought to the notice of their fathers;

and to the knowledge of My covenants which I made with the house of Israel, saith the Lord.

6 And again, a seer I will lift up of the fruit of thy loins, and I will give him power to carry My word to the seed of thy loins who were brought into this land beyond the sea and which are a remnant of the house of Manasseh and Ephraim, that is, to his brethren; and not only to bring to his brethren the words of his father, but to the convincing them of My word, which shall already have been declared unto them by the hand of the first seer of the last days.

7 And to this seer I will bless, and those who seek to destroy him will be confounded; because this promise I gave unto you because of the first seer in the fullness of time, on whom I promised that I would remember the fruit of his loins from generation after generation, even after that the arrow of death, a ray that I saw in the hand of the enemy's shot down the esteemed seer; and the name of his son shall be as his own, and it shall be Joseph, according to the name of his father; and he shall be like to you, Joseph of Egypt; and what the Lord make by him, shall lead My people in the latter days.

8 And the Lord swore to Joseph that He would keep his seed forever, saying: As I will raise up Moses in Egypt, that he may be a token of that which I will bring in the last days, having in his hand a rod to gather My people Israel, in the midst of a promised land, and having discernment according to the Spirit to write My words, but not many, for I will write My law by the finger of My own hand, on stone tablets, and I will prepare him a spokesman whose name shall be Aaron.

9 Behold, in the same way, I, the Lord, will raise up a Moses in the last days; and I will give him power over a rod; and the ability to write a record, but I will not let him speak much, for I will not untie your tongue; but I will write unto him My law by the finger of My hand, which are the records of the ancient prophets of this place, that

in this land overseas, My people will live by the teachings of a metal book.

10 Therefore, I will not make him powerful in words among those to whom he will carry this message, but I will write My law in your heart by the finger of My own hand; and I will prepare him a spokesman, as Aaron shall be to Moses; but this one will come from thy loins, My servant Joseph.

11 Behold, therefore, I, the Lord, will raise up a Moses for the preservation of the fruit of thy loins, and I will prepare for him a spokesman from thy loins. And, behold, I, the Lord, will make this one, a Moses, write the account that was left by the fruit of thy loins to the sons of men, and also to the knowledge of the fruit of thy loins; and the spokesman of thy loins shall declare to his people in the last days.

12 Behold, therefore, the words that this, a Moses, shall write, shall be the words which I, in My wisdom, deem fit[1] to come unto the fruit of thy loins in the fullness of times. And it shall be as if the fruit of thy loins cried out to them from the dust, that these words may rise again in the latter days; for I know their faith. And all thy seed shall cry out from the dust; yea, they will cry repentance unto their brethren that dwell upon the face of the earth, even after many generations have passed with the opening of these words unto the children of men. [1] **RLDS 2Nephi 2:38; Ether 2:1** / LDS 2Nephi 3:19; Ether 5:1

13 And because of their faith, behold, the words of this one Moses, shall come forth out of My mouth unto their brethren, which are the fruit of thy loins; and of the weakness of his words, for behold, he shall not be able to speak, but I will strengthen him by his faith, so that the covenants which I have made with thy fathers can be remembered concerning the gifts of My Spirit in the last days.

14 And because of this covenant you are blessed; for thy seed shall not be destroyed, for they shall hearken unto the words of the book that this, a Moses, shall deliver unto his spokesman, in whose cry of repentance to his brethren shall be heard by many, even according to the simplicity of his words, same after many generations.

15 Until I, the Lord, raise up one thy brethren in the last days; yea, one mighty among them, who shall do much good, both in word and in deed, being an instrument in My hands, with exceeding faith, to work mighty wonders, and do that thing which is great in the sight of God, unto the bringing to pass much restoration unto the house of Israel, and unto the seed of thy brethren.

CHAPTER 13

The story of Moses before he left Egypt.

1 It happened then, that I, Moses, I was born in Egypt, in the same city that my ancestors lived from the time the Hebrews came to the land of Goshen, where there were the best pastures of the land of Egypt, at the invitation of Pharaoh — as it is written in the annals of the history of Israel, that Joseph, the ruler of Egypt, made his fathers and his brothers to dwell in the land of Rameses, the district of Goshen, just as Pharaoh had commanded him[1]. [1] Genesis 47: 11 – IV

2 And I am Moses, the son of Amram, grandson of Kohath, and the great-grandson of Levi. My mother, Jochebed, was the sister of Kohath. Being me, three years younger than my brother Aaron and six years from my sister, Miriam.

3 It happened, therefore, on account of my birth, that Satan stirred Pharaoh's heart, to put an end to all the newborn boys among the children of the Hebrews. — On this occasion I was concealed by my mother Jochebed for a period of three months, and afterwards I was placed in a papyrus ark among the reeds on the bank of the Nile, where I was found by the daughter of Pharaoh, who became my foster mother.

4 By the attitude of my sister Miriam, who stood in the way of the daughter of Pharaoh on this occasion, I became breastfed and instructed in the knowledge of the Hebrew God, by my mother of blood, Jochebed, who became employed as wet nurse of the daughter's of Pharaoh, who gave me the name of Moses, and so soon presented me to the high council of Egypt as his son, a gift from Hapi, who was considered to be the god of the waters of the Nile among the Egyptians.

5 Since then many legends have arisen among the Egyptians as to what would happen to the future of this boy taken from the waters by the will of the gods.

6 And being created as a member of the house of Pharaoh, I was instructed in all the wisdom of the Egyptians, and became acquainted with their beliefs; the many myths and symbolisms of their temples; rituals of magic and offerings to their gods.

7 But, behold, none of this seemed to me correct, since there is no priestly structure among them, centered on one God, the Creator of the heavens and the earth, as the Hebrews teach; but each god has a temple and a group of men and women dedicated to their own worship.

8 And it came to pass in those days, that my heart was greatly troubled because of the death of Pharaoh, and because his son was younger than I, Moses, who was the adopted son of the daughter of Pharaoh who had died; and with that, considered himself among the class of the high echelon and of the rulers of the Egypt, if should be I the greater regent over Egypt.

9 For this reason, the immediate priests of the throne arranged the marriage of my adoptive mother with her half-brother, who was only a young man, but by hereditary succession right he should assume the position of the father like Pharaoh, as was the custom among the sons and daughters of Pharaoh.

10 Therefore, after the union of my mother with her brother, who became the Pharaoh in his father's place; behold, he began to fear that I, Moses, the eldest son of the queen of Egypt, the same one who had nurtured from her youth a great expectation in what I would become; could in the future eventually take the place of his bastard son, obtained with one of his concubines, the throne of Egypt. And for this reason, calling the queen before the court of Egypt, and the high-priests-immediate, he named his son, who was only a child, as successor to the throne.

11 The Pharaoh did this with the intention of preventing his sister-wife from placing her adopted son on the throne of Egypt in future times, after an eventual death of the pharaoh.

12 But as soon as the Queen witnessed such an affront, she announced to the high priests the will of the gods concerning me, with the purpose of putting me on the throne of Pharaoh, instead of the bastard son of his brother, in case he should die.

13 Yet, Pharaoh felt increasingly threatened with my existence in the court of Egypt, that so soon, it was rumored that he intended to kill me.

14 Nevertheless, the court of Egypt, out of fear of the gods, accepted the idea that I, Moses, would assume the kingdom of Egypt instead of the bastard son of Pharaoh, should he die; for they truly believed in their legends and traditions that the birth of the baby on the banks of the Nile satisfied the interest of all the gods venerated by them, for how much the Hebrews were finishing building the warehouses of the city of Pithom and Rameses in the land of Goshen, and if it were not fulfilled such an errand upon which it had been rescued from the hand of Hapi, that the confederate gods would throw plagues on the bed of the Nile and they would end with their crops, and thus they would be of no use to any storehouses or reservoirs built to store food in all that region of Egypt, bringing with them dishonor and reproach in the sight of all the nations of the land of Pharaoh.

15 In turn, I, Moses, fearing to be put to death by Pharaoh, and for my knowledge of the one Hebrew God, and for my faith in Him, renounced the honor of being called the son of the daughter of Pharaoh, choosing since then, to be ill-treated with the people of God in the city of slaves, than to have temporary usufruct of sin and idolatry impregnated in the culture and traditions of the Egyptian people.

16 The Queen of Egypt, however, seeing that my decision was unchanging, appointed me as a slave to the flocks of Pharaoh in the pastures east of Goshen, that I should not suffer with the burdens laid upon the Hebrews who participated in the buildings in cities of Rameses and Pithom.

17 And it came about at dusk that I, Moses, went to my people among the buildings that were being erected at the command of Pharaoh, and I saw how the Israelites of that part of the city were forced to do heavy work, being dishonored by the Egyptian masters.

18 I also saw an Egyptian beating on an Israelite, known to my brother Aaron, who was present at the meeting of the elders the night before. Then, looking around, and seeing that there was no one there, I approached to argue with that Egyptian about the ill-treatment of Pharaoh's masters of works, to the Hebrew people, but, behold, he attacked me, causing me to kill him, with no such intention in my heart, and out of fear I hid his body in the sand.

19 The next day, however, I saw two Israelites fighting, and in order to reason with them, I asked the aggressor of the reasons that had caused him to mistreat his brother. To which the man replied, he terrified me the mind, why he expounded what I did with the Egyptian at the end of the afternoon of the previous day.

20 When I saw that everyone already knew, I assumed that Pharaoh also knew about the murder, and that he would soon demand my death. Evidently that day, when gathered together with the congregation of the alley, the elders of Israel announced that Pharaoh issued a decree to deliver Moses to the Egyptian authorities in order to be executed.

21 And it came to pass in the course of that night, that I made as much as I could, and I departed from Egypt, leaving all, and all behind, and went and dwelt in a foreign land, and came to lodge with the family of Jethro, a priest and shepherd in the land of Midian.

22 Over the years while I was in Midian I heard reports that the Pharaoh who wanted my death, who was the husband and brother of the Queen of Egypt, had passed away, and that the Queen herself had assumed the throne of Pharaoh, since her son-nephew was still too small to take such responsibility. Years later, news comes that this one took the scepter of ruler, coming to finally sit on the throne of his father.

23 And what was heard among the Kenyan merchants, a people who inhabited the land of Midian, but were not Midianites of lineage, was the most talked about rumor among the Hebrews who lived in Egypt, that the new Pharaoh gave orders to his craftsmen, so that the name of Moses and of Joseph and of other Hebrews that ruled with their ancestors, from the records of all the land of Egypt would be they extinguished.

24 Yea, of all the records of Egypt, and any record identifying a descendant of a slave as being the son of the Queen of Egypt; and everything that concerns a baby that has been rescued from the waters of the Nile, so that future generations will not recall that in ancient times the self-echelon of Egypt tried to put in the place of the Great Pharaoh, son of Ra, the descendant of a Hebrew slave, and never to make this a native Egyptian legend in association with the god Hapi.

CHAPTER 14

The story of Moses after he left Egypt.

1 So I established myself as the shepherd of Jethro's flock; a priest in the land of Midian, and who became my father-in-law, through his daughter Zipporah. I discovered that the Midianites were descendants of Abraham by Keturah; wife whom he married after Sarah died, and by whom Midian was born to him[1]. So I took knowledge that the descendants of Abraham, through their sons Ishmael and Midian, were for a long time very similar peoples in their way of worshipping the God of our ancestors, Abraham; Isaac, and Jacob, as are the Hebrews. [1] Genesis 25:1-6 – IV

2 And though Abraham commanded them to go into the east, far from the house of Isaac; before he died he gave gifts to Midian, and ordained him to the high priesthood of Melchizedek; just as he did to the other sons he had with his concubines; there being among the peoples that have derived of the seed from Abraham; a covenant with God through the priesthood of His Only Begotten Son; who was to remain active in his offspring, by promise, for how much were keepers of His commandments.

3 It happened then, at the time when I, Moses, dwelt in a foreign land, that I received from the hands of my father-in-law Jethro, then a priest in the land of Midian, the holy priesthood of Melchizedek. — This priesthood, which from generation to generation was passed down from father to son, from the days of Abraham to his generation. Being that Jethro was a righteous descendant of Abraham and a keeper of the commandments of God among the nomadic people he led. For how much the Midianite cities, had already become corrupted and fallen into apostasy.

4 However, when I came to know the priesthood powers with the elders of Midian, I realized that nothing was added to me, no gift, not even a spiritual realization beyond what my mind was capable of projecting. — I realized then that it was necessary to seek knowledge directly at the source, that is, with the God of Abraham; Isaac, and Jacob, or die looking for, because getting the priesthood did not make me better than I already was.

5 Many times during the day and sometimes at night, I would retreat in prayer in search of this God who did not even have a name, for from the days of my childhood when I began to hear about Him, I learned that it was not possible for the tongue of man to pronounce the name of God. — Then to whom should I pray? How to call someone whose name can not be pronounced?

6 It was then, in the course of these days of trouble, that the Lord God appeared to me, Moses, for he led the flock to the western side of the wilderness, at the foot of Mount Horeb, when I heard a loud noise, like the sound of a thunderclap, as soon as I turned to see where the sound came from, I saw a light cross the sky, but it was not a fallen star, for, behold, she walked in a straight line and without speed.

7 As she landed about me, a soft light descended from the sky, while that strong light who stood above me, was slowly disappearing. Suddenly, the light that came down, the presence of the Lord, remained in the rays of light, as if it were burning the bush that was in front of me, doing separation between me and the Lord. — I perceived as if a fire were enveloping the bush, but, behold, its leaves and branches did not burn as I stared at this event.

8 Then I began to turn and approach of the bush in front of me, to see what the phenomenon was of the cause of that supernatural event before my eyes, it was then that a voice came out of the middle of the burning bush, and calling me by name, twice consecutively, ordered me that I not come near to inspect the place, but even the shoes of my feet were to be left behind, claiming that the ground on which I was treading was sacred.

9 And as soon as He told me these words, He commanded me again, that I should take off the sandals and kneel before the burning bush, because the presence of God was before me.

10 And God spake unto me, saying: Behold, I am the God of your father, the God of Abraham, the God of Isaac, and the God of Jacob, your forefathers; and immediately I was filled with fear and trembling in the all of my being, and I cast my face to the ground; for I was afraid to look upon the face of God, and to die, as the elders of Midian related unto me, that no man could see God and still live.

11 And God said: Obviously I have seen the affliction of My people in the land of Egypt, and I heard their cry because of the oppression of those who force them to work, for I know their pains, and for this reason I am coming down to deliver My people of the oppressive hand of Pharaoh and lead them to a good and spacious land; a land flowing with milk and honey; to the place of the Canaanites and of Hittites, and of Amorites, and of Perizzites, and of Hivites, and of Jebusites. These are those tribes who have been infected in your progeny by Anakiel and his rebellious angels, before they were all thrown into prison, when they made a pact with Satan on Mount Hermon, just after the waters of the Flood to dry.

12 For this reason, I will exterminate the seed of the tribes that dwell in the land of your inheritance; and behold, thy people Moses, shall return to mount Zion, which is under the dominion of the Amorites, who were installed at the command of Satan, when they arrived in this land, and found the pillar of the city of Enoch, which remained after the floods.

13 In view thereof, I will send you to Pharaoh, for the cry of My people has come to Me, and I have seen the oppression which the Egyptians oppress My people Israel. — Therefore I am sending thee before the face of Pharaoh, that you may deliver My people out of the bondage of Egypt.

14 I asked the Lord, what would I say to the children of Israel, if they asked me, who sent to free them, and what would I say if they asked me His name?

15 Then God answered me, saying: I AM THAT I AM. And this is what you should say to the children of Israel, I AM sent me to you.

16 For I make known to you My name, which I did not reveal to Abraham; Isaac and Jacob[1]. You therefore have knowledge that I AM the existence beyond any reason or cause; I AM the One who fills all things; who dwells in light inaccessible to men in the flesh, whom no man has seen or can see unless he is vivified in the spirit[2], neither can the tongue of man utter My name. Therefore, I AM and I am in you and you are in Me through the feelings that emanate from My name. [1] Exodus 6:3 | [2] 1Timothy 6:16; RLDS D&C 67:3b; D&C 22:7b-7c / LDS D&C 67:11: Moses 1:11

17 Behold, therefore, that I give beginning, through you, to erect My church among My people Israel, for thou art a seer, having all the gifts that are conferred upon the head of the church. — Therefore, thou shalt be the voice of God unto My people, for from thy own mouth I, the Lord, will speak to them.

18 And, behold, I will give thee Aaron thy brother, the one that I'm bringing for you with some of the elders of the house of Israel; and Aaron will be your spokesman. Therefore, he must be ordained a prophet before the elders of the house of Israel, for how much he will speak these words of mine that will flow out of your mouth when you come to Egypt.

19 And when My people Israel accept your call, then you will have a church to command beyond the Jordan, where I will give you a land flowing with milk and honey. — Therefore I will make you commandments by which the people of the covenant will be governed, and all of them, I the Lord will baptize under a cloud, that all may enter into the covenant that I am making with all the nation of Israel in their wholeness.

20 You, therefore, have a great challenge, to lead the people of Israel to live righteously, according to My words after you leave Egypt. Then it came to pass that I, Moses, answered God, saying that the children of Israel would never believe in me, nor obey my voice, and mock me, because I tell them that the Lord appeared to me, but they do not have much esteem for me.

21 Then the Lord told me that for this reason he was sending Aaron as My spokesman, for he is held in high esteem among the elders of the house of Israel and among all the people of Jacob, and for this reason they will obey his voice.

22 However, the Lord transmuted my adverse feelings, but righteous by the zeal of the Lord, into a snake that He commanded me that to do, throwing my rod to the ground. After that, my body was filled with leprosy, so that the Lord taught me that this is how the priesthood power of His son it works in the men, and that according to my feelings I can interact with the physical elements of the earth and with my own body, because all nature groans and also awaits the release of the sin to which Adam's error was subjugated, because the earth itself and its elements were also cursed with the fall[1]. [1]

Romans 8:19-22

23 But behold, since the elements are arranged by the gifts, which are feelings derived from the name of God in me, they are grouped by the power of faith, which, through command of the word of God, the worlds were created; and so all creation submits to the authority that is in the name of God and of His Only Begotten Son, through the order of His priesthood, for the sake of His own deliverance.

CHAPTER 15

The story of Moses after returning to Egypt.

115

1 And the LORD spake unto Moses, saying: Go now and take your wife and her children, and return into Egypt; for the Pharaoh that ordered your death, hath died a long time, and all his officers that were commanded to take your life were buried with him. When you return, however, make sure that you do all the wonders that I have put in your hand in front of Pharaoh, saying to him: Thus saith the LORD; Israel is My son, My firstborn.

2 And it came to pass, that Aaron, my brother, came to meet me in the wilderness, as the LORD had told me. And it came to pass that I, Moses, went and reported unto Aaron all the words of the Lord, and all the signs which he commanded me to do.

3 And I, Moses, and Aaron, we left together with the elders of that place, and when we came into Egypt, all the elders were gathered together in one place, to hear from Aaron's mouth all the words that the Lord spoke to Moses. And behold, I, Moses, did the signs required for God before the eyes of the people who were with us at that day, and the people believed, and heard that the Lord had visited the children of Israel, and seen all their affliction; and together they bowed, and prayed in thanks to God.

4 It was then, when I, Moses, and Aaron, we first entered in the presence of Pharaoh, saying that Jehovah, the God of Israel, asks Pharaoh for the liberation of the Hebrew people to commemorate a festival of worship to their God in the wilderness for the period of three days, and Pharaoh assumed his air of grandeur and arrogance and did not recognize Him as God, stating that Jehovah had no authority over the gods of Egypt, nor any power before the son of Ra, to effect an act of deliverance from the Hebrews or any other ethnic group that was under Pharaoh's care.

5 Then it came to pass, that from the first sign, which Aaron made before Pharaoh, when I, Moses, said, Take up his staff and cast it to the ground, and the staff became a great snake. — But Pharaoh called Jannes, who was the chief priest of the wise men and the sorcerers; and Jambres[1], who was the master of the magical priests of Egypt; and they did the same thing with their magic from the occult knowledge coming from the order Mahan, which had been restored with the ascension of Egypt by the hand of Satan. [1] 2Timothy 3:8

6 Each of them threw his own staff on the ground, and they also turned into great snakes; and even though Aaron's staff had swallowed up the snake of the high priests, yet Pharaoh's heart was hardened, for he saw nothing mighty that Jehovah the Hebrew God could do that his own magicians would not do double.

7 Then the Lord spoke to me again and said: "Pharaoh's heart is insensible to the facts, for how much he keeps an air of superiority to Me, the Lord. — Behold, therefore, I, the Lord, will overthrow all his arrogance, and will not destroy him until he knows that there is no God but Me, and that no one can equal Me in all the earth[1]. [1] Exodus 9:15-16

8 And for this reason I will leave Pharaoh to exist, to show him My power, and that My name, Jehovah, may be known in all the nations that are under the sun because of Egypt. — Therefore, Pharaoh will still refuse to let My people go.

9 In turn, for how much the magician priests continue to deceive their hearts with priestly deeds of the Mahan order, I, the Lord, will multiply My signs in the land of Egypt.

10 So go again in the presence of Pharaoh in the morning, when he is going forth to go to the Nile, and you should touch the waters of the river with your rod, that it may become blood before the sight of Pharaoh; and though their wizards do the same, they will soon see that the power of the God of the Hebrews is overwhelmingly superior; for I am hurting not only the waters of Pharaoh's bath, but the wealth of Egypt, which depends exclusively on the Nile.

11 Then the Egyptians will ask Pharaoh: "Where is Hapi, the god of the waters of the Nile, he fled before Jehovah, or did he never exist, as Moses has taught among the Egyptians?"

12 Later, when the third plague occurred, even the magician priests were obliged to admit that "the finger of the Hebrew God was afflicting Egypt," and were so severely afflicted by the plague of boils that they could not appear before Pharaoh to oppose Moses during this plague.

13 Then came the frogs to ruin them; the locusts that devoured their crops, the hail and rain of stone and lightning that devastated their flocks; and the armies of angels[1], to bring calamity, slaying all the firstborn of Egypt, including the son of Pharaoh. From the fourth blow upon Egypt, Jehovah specifically separated Goshen to remain unscathed — setting aside the land where his people lived[2]. [1] Psalms 78: 49 | [2] Exodus 8: 22; 9: 26

14 After the time of the plagues, and the deliverance of the people of Israel by mighty hand, as recorded in the annals I wrote, the time has come when the Lord requires me, Moses, to structure His church so that the Lord would have a people with His name, by which He might call His special property among the children of men.

15 But because of being a complaining people, the Lord did not authorize me to call any of them under the priesthood of Melchizedek, for they were not worthy to be part of this holy order, except the twelve whom I appointed to send, and the rulers of a thousand; of one hundred; fifty-ten, but they have not been able to maintain this active craft because of their integrity, save Joshua.

CHAPTER 16

The story of Moses after freeing the Hebrews from slavery to Egypt.

1 It was then, at the crossing of the sea, under the cloud of the mighty God, that the nation of Israel, together with the Egyptians who had forsaken their land to serve Jehovah, underwent a baptismal process in me, Moses, through the cloud and of the sea, and became thus the "children of covenant" under the laws which the Lord God would give to me, for the purpose of teaching the children of Israel to live their commandments, as being a united people, which had just left behind the idolatry for the purpose of worshiping only the one true God, under the unity of the church that had been organized on the day of the Passover, before Israel left Egypt.

2 Regardless of where they were, they would all be one in the knowledge and subservience to the covenants made by Jehovah with the nation of Israel, from before they left Egypt, when all shared the Passover, fourteen days after the first new moon appeared in the heavens, which should be strictly observed according to the covenant established for liberation of the people of Israel, prefiguring then, that the Israelite nation, by observing the commandments given by me, Moses, would prefigure the "Church of the Lamb of God" in all dispensations. — For how much this one paschal day, to be observed strictly fourteen days after the first new moon of the first month Abib[1], is to be kept in perpetuity among the people of the covenant, because it represents the liberation of His people from the slavery of Egypt. However, it is also the first day that God organized His church from the beginning of time, and only on this day does God redeem it, whenever necessary, in every predetermined time by Him before the foundation of the world. [1]

Exodus 12:2, 6; 13:4

3 This being the terms predetermined by God to organize His church properly on the face of the earth, just as it occurred on the day of the first Passover observed by the Hebrews in Egypt on the fourteenth day of the month Abib. — However, the day when God established His church in the days of Adam, He set a fixed and unchanging day for the children of men, regardless of the position of the moon in the heaven; to which He set out in all ages to properly organize and structure His church on earth, and which by chance to occur on the fourteenth day of the lunar calendar among the people of Israel in Egypt, making this day for to be remembered for they, of generation after generation, but which for God, does not change the fixed day[1] decreed by Him and His Only Begotten before the foundation of the world and for all eternity. [1] RLDS D&C 17:1a-1b; Mormon 1:65 / LDS 20:1-2; Mormon 3:2

4 If, therefore, a church is organized to the Lord on a day other than this day, then this will serve as a Sign for you to know that this church does not proceed from the hand of God and that He will never lay its foundations on another day, beyond from the one who was predetermined from the beginning of all times.

5 It happened then, over time, because of the murmurings of all the congregation of Israel, that the disbelief of the people displeased the Lord, in view of all that He had done hitherto. And for this reason the Lord allowed our enemies to make war against us, to once again manifest to the people of Israel from whence their strength and their help came.

6 And it came to pass in the land of Rephidim, that the Amalekites encamped about to attack the children of Israel. In view of this, I, Moses, called Joshua and I commanded that he choose some men for the battle against the Amalekites; for how much I said to Joshua that I would be on the top of the hill according to the command that God had given me, in which I would hold the rod of the Most High in my two hands, while my arms would be in the high.

7 And thus said the Lord to me: Just as I live, if you keep your arms outstretched over your head, so shall thy victory be against Amalek tomorrow.

8 And Joshua did as I had told him, for how much I, Moses, Aaron and Hur, we climbed to the top of the hill. But, being me advanced in years, I could not bear to remain for a long time with my arms outstretched over my head with that heavy stick in my hands.

9 And as soon as I lowered my arms to rest, Amalek was immediately to take over the battle; but when I lifted up the rod, Israel prevailed against the Amalekites.

10 At this, Aaron and Hur interrupted me, saying, "It is seen by us that your hands Moses, are too heavy to keep your arm raised high; please let us help you." But behold, it had not been said by God that I might have help, and so I rebuked them at first.

11 But there came a time when I could no longer raise my hands to the top, and my legs could no longer stand, when Aaron and Hur came to sustain me; And they took a stone, and put it under me; and Aaron and Hur maintained my hands raised high, Aaron on the right side, and Hur on the left side; and so my hands stood firm until sundown. As a result, Joshua defeated Amalek and his people with the edge of the sword.

12 And it came to pass, when Jethro my father-in-law came to me, Moses, and my sons and my wife, Zipporah, in the wilderness to the mountain of God, where he was encamped; and as soon as I saw them, I immediately went out to meet my father-in-law, and bowed, and kissed him, and after asking each other about their well being, we went into my tent, where I told my father-in-law what Jehovah had done to Pharaoh and the Egyptians because of Israel, and all the tribulations that passed in the way, and how the Lord delivered us out of the hand of Amalek with the help of Aaron and Hur.

13 And it came to pass, upon my resistance to accept the help of Aaron and Hur, that the Lord said to me the next day: It is not good that I should stand alone in the presidency of church of My Firstborn, for how much you need support, just as I showed you in the battle of Rephidim, when Aaron and Hur helped you with high hands.

14 Behold now, I'll let you know, Moses; that there would be no victory if you had not allowed Aaron and Hur to sustain you at that moment. In a similar way I tell you: Behold, the time has come for you to organize My church according to the old order of Enoch, which has been in existence since the days of Adam, for how much My gospel is ever the same, being eternal and unchanging.

15 My gospel, therefore, must contain in itself all the offices of My priesthood, according to the old order of Enoch, even as I will make thee known through My servant Reuel, thy father-in-law.

16 And Jethro, when he heard these words of mine, behold, rejoiced for all the good that the LORD had done to Israel, and said: Blessed be the Lord who delivered you from the hands of the Egyptians and from the hand of Pharaoh; and, behold that now I know that the Lord is greater than all the gods, for in that in which the Egyptians exalted their gods, the Lord overcame them.

17 And it came to pass on the morrow, that my father-in-law saw all that I did unto the people, and said: Behold, it is not good for you to continue like this, but surely you must do as God has revealed to you. — But hearken unto the voice of him whom God hath appointed thee to hear, and I will counsel thee, and God shall be with thee.

18 Be you the leader of the people before God; and teach them the statutes and the laws of their church, and make known unto them the way in which they should walk, and the work which they ought to do; and of thy people Moses, seek out able men, fearful of God, men that cherish the truth, who hate covetousness; and designate them under your hands to offices of Elder, each according to what the Spirit of God shall direct thee, and thou shalt give him functions in the physical administration of the people of God through the lesser priesthood, and give the positions of spiritual administration of the congregation of Israel through the greater priesthood.

19 And since the people are very numerous, appoint officers in priesthood of Melchizedek to take care spiritually of the congregation, which you will call of rulers; yea, rulers of a thousand, rulers of a hundred, rulers of fifty, and rulers of ten; that they may judge this people at all times; but every serious cause, bring it to you, and every little cause they will judge according to the knowledge that they will obtain through you.

20 And it came to pass, that I, Moses, did all that my father-in-law had said. Beginning with him, when I ordained him to the position of Patriarch, for he was already high priesthood[1]. After ordaining him to the patriarchal office, I summoned Aaron, as my immediate counselor, because he stood beside me in the battle of Amalek, holding one of my arms, and as soon as I called as second counselor in the presidency of the church of the Lamb, Hur, for remaining on my left. Representing thus, each in his calling, my right arm and my left arm in the spiritual administration of the covenant people. [1]
Exodus 18:1 – IV

21 Over time, I have chosen many capable men from all over Israel, and I set them for heads over the people; rulers ones of a thousand, rulers of hundred, rulers of fifty, and rulers of ten; and they judged the people in small things according to the law of God. But the great ones left for me, Moses, to Judge.

22 I appointed twelve apostles afterward, whom I sent to the promised land to return to the covenant people with glad tidings; I also appointed seventy according to the ancient order established by God from the beginning of the world in the likeness of the heavenly order, in common accord with the church of the Firstborn. And so I instituted among the people of Israel in my day, the church of the lamb of God, with all their offices properly organized.

CHAPTER 17

)f Moses before the council of the heavens.

1 And it came to pass in the third month after we left the land of Egypt, that we came to Sinai on the same day of the new moon, and after all the congregation of Israel set up a camp at the foot of the mountain, behold, on the third day, I went up the mountain to meet the Only God and from the mountain Jehovah said to me: Thus you shall say to the house of Jacob and to the children of Israel; your own eyes have seen what I did to the Egyptians; and now if you will obey My voice and obey My covenant, you will be My personal treasure among all the nations, and I will make you a Kingdom for Me. You will therefore be a kingdom of priests and a holy nation.

2 Therefore, under the cloud of the Almighty, I obtained the necessary instructions to organize the tabernacle of Israel for the full worship of the church of the Lamb in the wilderness. It was when the Lord caught up me again, and I, Moses, obtained the information concerning this book, which should remain sealed until God judges it prudent[1] to reveal these things to the children of men, when the Lord shall raise up a Moses like me[2], in the figurative sense, for he will be taken from among the nations, from a land that does not correspond to the covenant made by God with His people in the fullness of time, but this one whom God chooses, he will be sent to proclaim repentance to this people in the last days. **[1] RLDS 2Nephi 2:38; Ether 2:1** / LDS 2Nephi 3:19; Ether 5:1 | **[2] RLDS D&C 22:24b**/ LDS Moses 1:41-42

3 On this occasion I had the most astonishing privilege any man had ever had before. In preparation for what the Lord had told me; he led the children of Israel to the foot of the mountain on the morning of the third day, thunders, and thunderbolts, and they sounded from the top; and the sound of a trumpet sounded, announcing the coming of the Almighty.

4 The whole camp was filled with smoke, for the Lord had come down in a great chariot of fire; there was a cloud around the chariot and rays of light pierced the fog in the sight of all Israel's nation, for how much it was possible to be seen through the fog, God sitting on His throne, under a polished layer of fine amber which stretched upon itself. — But behold, when the children of Israel came so close, God commanded me to go back to them and warn them to not come so close to something that they can not touch; even same the priests; for the people had not yet consecrated all things in a united order, just as the people of Enoch did in former times.

5 Therefore, they could not bear the command that said, "Even an animal, if it touches the sacred mountain, must be stoned to death; then, as I, the Lord, will spare him who profanes My sanctuary?"

6 Behold, I, Moses, am not pleased with the lack of reverence of this people for My presence and their evil mores is an insult to Lord, their Creator. For up there in the mountain, Jehovah laid His hand upon me, and conferred upon me the keys of the dispensation which I should preside over. And he carried me to a very high mountain, above the clouds, until I came to the city of God, the Heavenly Jerusalem.

7 It was then, that I came to see something so impressive, that I, Moses said: "I am trembling with fear my God!" And the Lord said: What you see is the mount Zion, and unto the city of the living God, the heavenly Jerusalem, with His thousands of angels round about.

8 And, behold, it is given unto you permission to participate in the assembly of the elder sons of God, which is the church of the Firstborn of the Father; that is, of those who already have their names written in heaven. To you, Moses, it will be permitted to watch God presiding at a universal conference, for purposes, to determine the reward of the just spirits that have been perfected in the world, and you will see the Only Begotten Son of the Father, yea, the mediator of the new covenant, through whom you can be perfected[1]. [1] Hebrews 12: 21-24

9 Then it came to pass, that on this occasion I, Moses, saw God as one man sees another before his eyes, and God, face to face, spoke with me, and the glory of God was upon me; therefore, I, Moses, could bear His presence[1], although at no time did I dare raise my eyes to see His face. Therefore, God added, saying: Behold, you, Moses, having the priesthood power of My Son and being in accord with His ordinances, may look directly into My face with your eyes; though no man can see My countenance and remain alive without this priesthood. [1] 1Timothy 6:16; RLDS D&C 67:3b; D&C 22:7b-7c / LDS D&C 67:11: Moses 1:11

10 When you came here, I told you to sit in the place that I prepared for you, in the sacred mountain of meeting, and I ordered you to remain seated while My Glory passed between the rock of My throne. And, behold, I laid My hand upon the cleft of the rock that divided between Me and thee, and covered thine eyesight to not see My countenance, and then when I withdrew My hand, and you looked over your shoulder and saw Me at a glance behind you, giving you the keys of the administration of My priesthood; for how much My face can not be seen for lack of this seal that I put about thee.

11 For, behold, the priesthood does allow man to see God, provided that this man has received the key corresponding to such a privilege and is a high priest of the sacred order of the Only Begotten Son, possessing all the keys corresponding to his ministry, which was preordained from before the foundation of the world.

12 But this mystery, My son Moses, which I make known to you at this time, concerning the hundred and forty-four thousand high priests anointed by Me on Mount Zion, in the Heavenly Jerusalem, even before the foundation of the world; chosen among all nations of the earth, from among all times by Me predetermined, beginning with its dispensation, from which My people Israel shall be scattered throughout the four corners of the world.

13 Therefore, these high priests, remnants of the twelve tribes of Israel, must know this mystery to remain only among those who possess this gift and calling, or among those to whom I, the Lord, allow this mystery to be revealed to him through a high priest born in the world of mankind in the similarity of Melchizedek.

14 And God went on speaking to me, Moses, saying: Behold, I am the Lord God Almighty; and Infinite is My name, for I am without the beginning of days or the end of years; and is not that infinite?

15 Being that you are My son; behold, I am pleased to show thee the works of My hands; but not all, because My works have no end, nor My words, because they never cease. Behold, therefore, that no man shall be able to see all My works, without contemplating all My glory; and no man can contemplate all My glory and then remain in the flesh upon earth.

16 And it came to pass, while the voice still spoke, I looked and saw the earth; yea, all of it; and there was not a particle of it which I saw not, discerning it by the Spirit of God. And I have also seen inhabitants; and there was not a single soul that I had not seen, and his number was great, even as countless as the sands of the shore.

17 And I saw many lands; and each was called the world, and there were inhabitants on its surface; then I understand who were the righteous spirits who had been perfected in the heavens; and I was able to understand, who were those ancient spirits who made up the church of the Firstborn and I could understand who are the high priests who were ordained by God before the foundation of the world of mankind and because they have been endowed with knowledge since they are born.

18 These have been anointed with the knowledge of all things from the beginning, not needing anyone to teach him something about the Kingdom of God[1], but being from infants endowed with such divine attributes, they feel the desire to serve God and seek from Him the knowledge, for how much to these, will be shown the way to which they must walk before God. [1] 1 John 2:24-27

19 And it came to pass that I cried unto God, saying: Tell me, I beseech thee, why are these things so, and by what manner have ye done them? — And the Lord God said to me: "Moses, I have done these things for My own purpose. Here is wisdom, and abideth in Me; it also continues in you, and through you, and through those whom I call, for how much I call no man, unless they get elected; for not even My own Only Begotten was chosen by Me, but this one, being with Me from the beginning, acting as master of works of all creation, elected himself, saying, "Father, here am I; send Me."

20 And by the word of My power I have created all things; word which proceeds from Me, the Great Jehovah and Judge of all the earth[1], that since the days of Adam is pronounced "Almighty God", whose name is personified by election in the Only Begotten Son, this Jehovah being the Advocate with the Father[2], who from time immemorial is pronounced – "Mighty God", who is full of grace and truth. [1] RLDS Moroni 10: 31 / LDS Moroni 10: 34 | [2] RLDS - Visions of Joseph and Oliver in Kirtland Temple (RCH 2:46-47) / LDS D&C 110: 3-4

21 And I have created countless worlds; and also created them for My own purpose; and created them by the Son, who is My Only Begotten; and I called Adam the first man of all men, that is, many. However, I'll tell you only of this Earth and its inhabitants. For behold, there are many worlds which by the word of My power have passed away, as the world of mankind is passing now, but he that doeth My will, these standeth for ever. And there are many who now stand and are innumerable for man to understand; but all things are understandable to Me, for they are mine and I know them in detail.

22 And it came to pass that I, Moses, spake unto the LORD, saying: Be merciful to thy servant, O God, and tell me concerning this earth, and to the inhabitants, and to the heavens; and then your servant will

128

be satisfied. And, behold, the Lord God spake unto me, saying: The heavens are many, and are innumerable for a man to comprehend in his fullness; even as a land shall pass away, and her heaven shall be dissolved, so that another in her place shall arise; and there is no end to My works or My words.

23 Yet, behold, this is My work and My glory: To bring to pass the immortality and eternal life of man. And now, Moses My son, write these things which I will tell you at this time: for in the day when the children of men shall despise My words, and shall take away many of them from the book which thou shalt write, behold, I will raise up another like unto thee; and they will again be within reach of the children of men by these things that you record now — so that these words of mine may find all those who believe in My everlasting gospel, that this knowledge which will be revealed by this man whom I will raise up in the last days, like you, will gather again those who belong to Me, for they are My elect to support this My work and restore the heritage of My people in the final part of the fullness of times.

24 Thus, in the face of thunders and lightning and sounds of the trumpets proceeding from the heavens, Jehovah the Almighty made me deliver His law with a sublime display of authority, so that not only the nation of Israel would know that He is the only true God and alive over the sons of men, but that His people in every dispensations may know that there is no God besides Him, and as He has placed full trust in the nation of Israel throughout all his generations, keeps this record under seal, so that His chosen in the last days, by whose priesthood essence, which gifts of God, wrapped in the sentiments of the children of men, manifest among the people of His church in the final part of the fullness of times.

25 Behold, I am Mormon, son of Mormon, and a descendant of Nephi, and these are the words that I summarized from the record of the great Moses that God commanded me to write them according to my way of speaking; which were written and preserved for a wise purpose foreordained by God in the last days.

26 Behold, this is all that God commanded me to extract from the record of Moses, for the purpose of compiling on the plates I am transcribing, in which I am making a complete account of the things required for God, to be sealed in two stages, these words of Moses, which will be revealed in the first stage in preparation for a deeper knowledge that unfolds with the opening of the other books that compose this set behind the first seals, which should be opened in preparation of a people for the coming of Christ in His temple; with the purpose of this people being prepared for when He comes upon Zion of the last days.

27 And unlike the days of Moses, when He came down upon the top of mount Sinai, whose people were not worthy to touch the mountain where the Lord stood by His servant Moses, His son Jesus Christ, will find at last, a people who observe His commandments, strictly clean from the filthiness of the world of Satan and pure of heart; having all things in common, just as in the days of Enoch, when they lived in a 'united order.' — Amen.

28 I, Mormon, being impressed by the reading of a passage from this record of Moses, whereby, reading his words, the Holy Spirit did not require me to compile such an epilogue from the twelve spies, to compose the outcome of this record on the plates that I am transcribing.

29 However, after concluding what the Lord actually asked of me, I began to beg the Lord that the story of the spies of Moses, who were sent, one from each tribe of Israel, therefore the twelve apostles, to bring good tidings of the earth promised to the children of Israel, may also be written by me, Mormon, here on these plates.

30 It follows, therefore, as it appears in its details in the record of Moses. Only understanding this stretch is enough for anyone to understand the power of human feelings and the extent that connects us to gifts from the name of God. Amen.

The Twelve Apostles of Moses and the Promised Land

1 And God spake unto me, Moses, and said: Separate a man from each tribe; righteous men, and honorable men, and princes of his people, to send them into the land of Canaan. Therefore shall your ambassadors be appointed to keep watch over the land which I shall give to the children of Israel for an inheritance, and to make a report for the purpose of each of these princes represent their tribe before all the people, when they report in a general assembly between the nation of Israel all the good things that proceed from this place; for, behold, I am giving unto you for an inheritance a land flowing with milk and honey.

2 These are their names: Of the tribe of Reuben, Shammua, son of Zaccur; of Simeon, Shaphat the son of Hori; of Judah, Caleb the son of Jephunneh; of Issachar, Igal, the son of Joseph; of Ephraim, Hosea son of Nun; of Benjamin, Palti the son of Raphu; of Zebulun, Gaddiel the son of Sodi; of Joseph, by the tribe of Manasseh, Gaddi the son of Susi; of Dan, Ammiel the son of Gemalli; of Asher, Sethur the son of Michael; of Naphtali, Nahbi the son of Vophsi; of Gad, Geuel the son of Machi.

3 These are the men whom I, Moses, sent to spy out that land; and to Hoshea the son of Nun, I, Moses, gave the name of Joshua.

4 It came to pass, that I, Moses, commanded that every one of them should observe the people that dwell in it; whether they were strong or weak; whether they were few or many. Whether their cities were fortified or not; whether the land was fertile or withered; if there were trees and beds of rivers.

5 So the twelve went up, and when they returned they brought with them a cluster of grapes, for it was the days of the firstfruits, where the grapes came forth. And, behold, these grapes were so great, that it was necessary, two men with a staff piercing the bunch to carry them.

6 And at the end of the forty days since they left, they stood before Moses and Aaron, and all the congregation of the children of Israel, and began to tell them what they saw, and to show them the fruits of the land.

7 And they said unto them: We have gone into the land which thou hast sent us; and truly flowed with milk and honey as the Lord said to His servant Moses. See, this is its fruit. Behold, the people marveled at the quality and size of the grapes, and were filled with enthusiasm by the account of Caleb and Joshua.

8 But the ten other spies reported to them, saying: Behold, the people that dwell in the land are mighty, as we have heard of the Nephilim, who were the children of Anak before the flood, and their cities are exceedingly fortified, and very great. Beyond these are the Amalekites that dwell in the land of the south; and the Hittites, and the Jebusites, and the Amorites that dwell in the mountain; and the Canaanites that dwell by the sea, and by the river Jordan.

9 And it came to pass that Caleb shut up the people, saying: Let us go up quickly, and take this land for an inheritance; because we will surely prevail against it and get the best that exists in all the regions around us.

10 But the rest of the men who watched over the land said: "Why, Caleb, do not be naive, for we can not go up against that people, for they are stronger than we are." Behold, there is nothing good for us in that place, for the land which we have passed through to spy is a land that consumes its inhabitants; and all the people that we see in it are men of great stature; yea, we saw there giants, sons of Anak, as our ancestors told us, that they existed before the flood. But we testify that the descendants of the giants still exist; and we are like locusts in front of them.

11 And all the congregation arose, and lifted up their voice; and the people wept that night. And it came to pass, that all the children of Israel murmured against me, Moses, and against Aaron my brother; and all the congregation lifted up their voice and said: Tell us now, Moses, why does the Lord bring us to this land, that we may fall by the sword, and that our wives and children be preys of giants? —It would have been better if we had died in Egypt.

12 And it came to pass, that Joshua, the son of Nun, and Caleb, the son of Jephunneh, rent their clothes; and they spake unto all the congregation of the children of Israel, saying: The place whither we go to is a very good land. If we do not rebel against the Lord and not fear the people of the land, then the Lord will be with us. And, behold, just as He delivered us out of Egypt with an outstretched arm, so He will bring us into the land of giants, and He will give us for an inheritance a land that truly flows with milk and honey.

13 And it came to pass, when the congregation proceeded to gather stones to stone Joshua and Caleb; the Glory of the Lord appeared upon the congregation of the children of Israel, and the LORD said to Moses: How long will this people provoke Me? And how long will they not believe Me, in spite of all the signs I have made among them?

14 Therefore, the Lord said: At no time did I command you that the twelve men who had inspected the promised land should report the bad things of this land to the people of Israel, but that they should only report on the good things that are there.

15 Understanding, then, the key point to which the Lord intended to arrive in relation at the negative feelings of His servants, I, Moses, said: Behold, I am but a mortal man to argue with Almighty God; but if thou slay this people which thou broughtest out of Egypt as one man, then the rest of the nations that have heard of thy fame shall say: The God of the Hebrews could not set this people in the land which had sworn to them; therefore He slew them in the wilderness.

16 Now therefore, I beseech thee, God, let the strength of my Lord magnify himself before the people of all the earth. Therefore, forgive the iniquity of thy people, according to the greatness of Thy mercy, and as thou also hast forgiven this people from the land of Egypt up to here because of their grumbling and their evil feelings that are impregnated in their hearts by reason of their parents who were bitter by generation after generation like slaves in Egypt, in such a way, that you can not uproot those feelings in a single moment, but patience is required with your people Israel.

17 And speaking to me, the Lord said: According to thy word, Moses, I have forgiven them. But I swear by Myself, that these, which thou hast declared to be impregnated with evil feelings, which shall fill the heart of this people with feelings malignant, shall not see the land which I swore to their fathers.

18 But My servant Caleb, because there was another spirit in him, that is, there was another kind of feeling in his heart, and he persevered in following Me, keeping with him the faith which he obtained through the power that came from Me in Egypt; behold, I, the Lord, will bring him into the land where he went in to spy, and his seed shall possess it for an inheritance; from generation to generation.

19 And the LORD spake unto me, Moses, and Aaron, saying: I have heard the murmurings of the children of Israel since they came out of Egypt, with their feelings of displeasure toward Me, the Lord. — How long shall I endure this evil congregation, which murmureth against Me in your feelings?

20 Behold, therefore, your carcases shall fall in this wilderness, as also all that were numbered of you according to all your number, from twenty years upward, which murmurest of you against Me in sentiments; for they shall not go into the land, by which I lifted up My hand with an oath, save Caleb the son of Jephunneh, and Joshua the son of Nun for the goodness of their hearts.

21 Of the remainder, even to their children, whom I will preserve under the age of twenty, I am taking away the greater priesthood, leaving among the children of Israel only the lesser priesthood, as a preparatory path of greater things.

22 Behold, ye are not worthy of such greatness, because I have desired to obtain a people for My name; a property that I could call My own; a nation of Priests, but these did not qualify in the days of Moses.

23 Behold, to this end I will continue to work, and at the end of all, when in the fullness of time I shall come, then I will find upon the earth a people ready to receive Me. Amen.

ACTS OF THE THREE NEPHITES

Written by Jonah, the son of Nephi, a disciple of Jesus, and given to Mormon at the time the three disciples ministered to me and my son, Moroni.

CHAPTER 1

1 When we try to understand God's proceedings from a human perspective, the rest of the story told to us looks a fable, unless God gives the children of men, according to their attention and diligence, to know its mysteries.

2 Concerning this, behold, it was prophesied by the prophets of old, that these records would be sealed; kept and preserved by the hand of the Lord until they were brought to the knowledge of all nations, tribes, tongues, and peoples, that they might know the mysteries of God contained therein.

3 And now, before you suppose that this is foolish; I want to remind you that there are many mysteries that remain hidden, which no one knows but God himself. And behold, it was by the wisdom of God that these records were preserved; with the purpose of increasing the knowledge of His people in the fullness of times; being an instrument in the hands of God to accomplish His great and eternal designs among the children of men.

4 Remembering still, that the foolishness presented by God in the course of all dispensations was the means by which the Lord confounded the wise men and teachers of the law among His people, to do His work among those who, according to the attention and diligence that if they dedicate, come to understand their mysteries, and to bring salvation to their souls.

5 Those, therefore, who do not harden their hearts when these records are finally revealed to the children of men, will be endowed with wisdom to understand the greater part of the word already revealed, until it is given to know the mysteries of God in its fullness. But those who harden their hearts when these records appear among them, even the knowledge they possess of the first set of books revealed, will become obtuse in their minds, until they know nothing of their mysteries.

6 This record, therefore, which is granted now to the children of men, is a great and important mystery of the mysteries of God, and for this reason you can not suppose in your intellect, that it be easy to understand, because the things written here do not follow the events in chronological order, but, as with all the other scriptures left to us by the ancient prophets, future events are set in front of the prevailing affairs, and then again to intertwine in the same plot of history that is being written the present and the past so that, according to the dictates of the heavens, this entanglement of information, will compose the substance of faith in the feelings of those whose heart is receptive to the word of God through the Holy Spirit.

7 So desire to remember what was said by Alma, that "faith is not perfect knowledge". The same is true of these words of mine. At first, you can not be sure of them until you awaken your spiritual faculties, testing the words of this record as a result of what was written by the ancient prophets, and exercise a particle of faith in your quest for knowledge of the mysteries of God, still though you only have the desire to know the truth behind my words, and let this desire operate in your heart and mind, until you comprehend the fullness of these mysteries, so that you may with all diligence add to your faith the virtue of this new perception.

CHAPTER 2

1 In prayer, touching the twelve disciples with the finger, Jesus gave each of us the promise of what we desired in our hearts, and with the exception of the three of us, all others wished to have an end in the ministry to which they were called and that after having lived the age that man is allowed to live, that they might soon go to Christ in His Kingdom. Nevertheless, the Lord blessed them because they desired this in their hearts; and after praying and sharing the bread and wine among the twelve, as Jesus taught, that this sharing ceremony of the bread and wine prefigures an ordinance of the Greater Priesthood that existed from the beginning of time at different times on earth; whenever the high priesthood of the son of God is active among the children of men, beginning with prophets and apostles of the church of the Lamb[1] in remembrance of the agreement made between the members of this high council with the Father; and the Son; and the Holy Spirit, even before the foundation of the world[2], concerning the great sacrifice proposed in the heavens, which was effected by our Lord Jesus Christ, for the benefit of all men who repent and exercise faith in Him. [1] **Sealed Book of Moses 9:1; RLDS Genesis 14:17-18 - IV** | [2] **RLDS Alma 9:68-10:3** / LDS Alma 13:5-11

2 Then, Jesus rose and girded His loins with a drying cloth, took the water which He had commanded Timothy to bring in a jar of half measure, and poured into the basin that I, Jonah, brought by reason of His request; and one by one He washed the feet of the twelve, consecrating them[1] and ordaining them as high priests[2] of the sacred order of Melchizedek in order to organize the Church, starting with city of Abundance, until filling the whole earth. Then warned us that when we shall consecrate and ordain other high priests to help us in the things concerning the church, that we must do it in the same way that He did to us. [1] **RLDS Alma 3:3** / Alma LDS 5:3 | [2] **Sealed Book of Moses 9:4; RLDS 85:39b; 45-46b** / LDS D&C 88:128; 138-141; **John 13:3-7**

3 And turning unto the three of us, He said unto us: Do not worry about that which ye desired in your hearts; behold, I know your thoughts; and you wished that which John My beloved, that hath followed Me in My ministry, desired Me.

4 Therefore, you are more blessed, for you will never taste the bitterness of death; but you shall live from generation to generation to see all the works of the Father among the children of men, till all things be fulfilled according to the will of the Father, when I will come in My glory with the powers of heaven among My people in Earth.

5 You, therefore, will never suffer the pains of death; but when I come in My glory, you will be transformed in the twinkling of an eye, from your mortality to immortality; and then shall ye be blessed in the kingdom of My Father; for how much you will not suffer the pains of death while ye abide in the flesh; except for the sins of the world; and all this I will do by virtue of what you have asked of Me, because you have desired to bring the souls of men to Me as long as the world exists.

6 Behold, for this reason you will have complete joy and sit in the kingdom of My Father; Yea, your joy will be complete, just as the joy that the Father has given Me is complete; and you will be like "I AM" in your hearts, because "I AM" as the Father; and the Father and I are interconnected by our feelings, just as you also will be bound to My name; and after He had uttered these words, Jesus laid His hands on us and departed.

7 And behold, the heavens were opened before us, and we were translated into heaven, and we have seen and heard unspeakable things, which it was forbidden for us to speak to the people of our day; nor was it given power to describe the things which we have seen and heard in that generation; and whether we were in the body or out of the body, we can not say; because we do not know what actually occurred to us except that we had been transfigured, as if we had been changed from that body of flesh to an immortal state in that instant, so that we could contemplate the things of God.

8 And, behold, as we return, we resume our ministry on earth; yet we did not reveal the things which we saw and heard to men in the flesh, because of the command given to us in heaven, but we were ordered to do this record[1] — that we go out by the face of the earth and minister among all the people, bringing to the church all who believed in our preaching; baptizing people who believed in our words, and all who were baptized received the Holy Spirit in confirmation of our ministry. [1] **RLDS 3 Nephi 13:29-30** / LDS 3 Nephi 28:18

9 And, behold, we shall be among the Gentiles and the Gentiles shall not know us. We will also be among the Jews and the Jews will not know us. And it shall come to pass, when the Lord shall deem expedient in His wisdom, then we three we will minister among all the scattered tribes of Israel, to gather together the remnant of the house of Jacob from all the nations, tribes, and tongues; and among them we will bring many souls to Jesus, that their desire may be satisfied; and also by virtue of the convincing power of God who is with us.

10 Yea, even among the Gentiles a great and marvelous work will be performed before the day of judgment, and then all the scriptures that relate the wonderful works of God, according to the words of Christ, will be revealed to the children of men, when then, Jesus comes over among His people in the fullness of times[1]. [1] **RLDS 3Nephi 13:45** / LDS 3Nephi 28:33

11 And woe unto them that will not hearken unto the words of Jesus, and to them which He hath chosen for to send before His coming; because those who do not receive the words of the books of those whom He will send to the Gentiles in the last days, do not receive it, and with this they will never obtain for themselves the words of the book that Jesus will reveal in the final part of the fullness of times.

Therefore, Jesus will not receive them on the last hour[1]. [(1)] RLDS 3Nephi 13:46-47 / LDS 3Nephi 28:34

CHAPTER 3

1 Around two hundred years since the coming of Christ among the Nephites, many of my people began to divide into classes, and began to organize churches for themselves, for the purpose of obtaining riches, prestige, and glory among their brothers.

2 It so happened that after two hundred and ten years had passed, that there were many churches professing to be the Church of Christ among my people, yet they suppressed most of their gospel, and modified the principal doctrines and ordinances to fit to a more liberal way of living, in such a way that they tolerated all sorts of iniquities and promiscuities because of the easy path their leaders presented to their members, because they get a profit by encouraging the people from setting aside the principles of equality between brothers, because until then the true Church kept all things in common among the members, each making profit in their business, but not for themselves, but for the collective good of all the brethren under the solemn covenant of the united order, according to his desires and needs.

3 And these churches multiplied greatly, because of the iniquity and power of Satan that took hold of their hearts to the point of rejecting our preaching, because we were among them. Nevertheless, they threw us into prison; but its walls could not withstand the power of God that was with us and as soon as we were chained in chains, the fetters were broken. We were thrown into the fire, but we emerged unharmed before their eyes; in wild animal pits, but we played with the beasts in the same way a child plays with a lamb; and we left without any scratch before the eyes of the multitude that observed us.

4 Nevertheless, the people hardened their hearts, and attacked the people of Jesus; but the people of Jesus did not retaliate against the attacks, because they obeyed His teaching, of not to throw your gifts before those who despise them. And so they were degenerating in unbelief and iniquity from year to year, until two hundred and thirty years passed; and then there was a great division among the people.

5 And it came to pass at the beginning of these days, that there arose a people called the Nephites, and they were true believers in Christ; and there were three distinct tribes among them, whom the Lamanites called Jacobites, and Josephites, and Zoramites; because of the three disciples of Christ, for we individually ministered, each among one of these tribes, from which we descended; and all the men, women, and children who formed the people of the Church were called Nephites; independent of the tribe they belonged to; being I, Jonah, a descendant of the tribe of Joseph, one of the sons of Nephi, who was the chief disciple of the Lord.

6 In this way, we instituted a single identification for the people of the church, without removing the tribes that composed them, so that their Church continued on the earth, just as in the days of our ancestors when they left Egypt. For although they were twelve distinct tribes, having different patriarchal designations from one another, they were recognized only by the peoples around, as the nation of Israel.

7 For how much we prevailed, the Church of Christ, after He was present among His people, as the Nephite nation, until two hundred and sixty years and the people of the Church began to become proud, by virtue of their great riches; to the point of the richest they no more be willing to share their profits with the poorest, because they already resented in dividing their assets; and were vain among their brethren, the Lamanites that congregated with us. And from then on,

142

we, the disciples, who were to remain on earth while there was the Church of Christ among the Nephites, began to suffer for the sins of the world.

8 Behold, here in this expression, "the disciples began to suffer for the sins of the world[1]" hides the great mystery of our ministry and existence among men on earth. For it was written by our poets and historians what was passed on to them by the culture of the peoples who lived with us during these two hundred and sixty years, having their children and their children's children heard some report from the past, of that we were brought to death more than once, but we were left unharmed in all cases. [1] RLDS 3Nephi 13:51 / LDS 3Nephi 28:38

9 Claiming, therefore, that on the occasion of our call to remain on this earth, Jesus Christ said that "we would never taste death," but the fact is that we were told on this occasion by the voice of the Lord that "if you die in Me, you will not taste the death[1]." [1] RLDS D&C 42: 12f / LDS D&C 42: 46

10 And because of these words also it is said to this day among the Nephites: "If they were mortal or immortal from the day of their transfiguration[1], nobody knows; for they themselves reported that they were caught up into heaven, but did not know whether they were cleansed from mortality to immortality[2], only argued among their acquaintances that their bodies have undergone a transformation[3] so that they do not prove the bitterness of death[4] every time they were thrown into the fire or stoned to perish. " Therefore, although we are killed at all times, we do not suffer the pains of death or their agonies; except "for the sins of the world[5]."

[1] RLDS 3Nephi 13:29 / LDS 3 Nephi 28:17 | [2] RLDS 3Nephi 13:49 / LDS 3Nephi 28:36 | [3] RLDS 3Nephi 13:50 / LDS 3Nephi 28:37 | [4] RLDS D&C 42:12f / LDS 42:47 | [5] RLDS 3Nephi 13:51 / LDS 3Nephi 28:38

11 I speak of this, because of the iniquity and unbelief that increased among the Nephite people from time to time, and of the many times that the three of us were taken out of the midst of the people and regarded as slain by those who knew us. This happened for the first time one hundred years after the coming of Christ, when all the disciples had already gone to the paradise of God except us three[1], but the whole first generation of those who saw Jesus had died[2]. [1]

RLDS 4Nephi 1:15-16 / LDS 4Nephi 1:14 | [2] RLDS 4Nephi 1:21 / LDS 4Nephi 1:18

12 My father was one of the disciples of Jesus Christ, the one who resurrected his brother Timothy[1], and who was still alive on the occasion of everyone already have died, except us three[2]. And the church was living a period of peace and justice among its people, but as soon as the Lord transferred us again, behold, one of my brethren gave continuity to our father's record. [1] RLDS 3Nephi 3:60; 9:4 /LDS 3Nephi 7:19; 19:4 | [2] RLDS 4Nephi 1:15-16, 22 / LDS 4Nephi 1:14, 19

13 Now, whether we die or not, we do not know for sure. Nevertheless, what happens to us is that we do not suffer the pains of death, which are forgetfulness when passing through the veil, but behold, we remember all things both in this dwelling and in the other, and so we must remain until all things be fulfilled, when then Jesus comes among His people in the last days, just as He came among the Nephites, and we will be transformed in the twinkling of an eye, of the mortality, that is, of this mortal state in which we are being delivered to death at all times, to immortality[1]. [1] RLDS 3Nephi 13:19 / LDS 3Nephi 28:8

14 And in this transitory state of being and not being in the world, we must remain, going and coming, in a partial and continuous transformation of what we are to be at the last day, so that Satan will not have power over us and so little acknowledge us among the children of men, and that we may not be held back by the rulers of the earth until the day of judgment, when we will then go through a complete transformation so that we may no longer leave the presence of God[1]. [1] RLDS 3Nephi 13:52-53 / LDS 3Nephi 28:39-40

15 Nevertheless, the lack of references by the ancient prophets in their writings to this procedure which Jesus Christ used with us, who

are the three disciples that should remain in the land, does not appear to exist in any previous account in the history of the gospel, from the beginning until now; except the account that was shown to us, when we were caught up, and we saw a book written by an apostle of the Lord, whose name was John; the one of whom the Lord Jesus had told us: "Behold, I know your thoughts, and you desire what John, My beloved, who has accompanied Me in My ministry before I was condemned by the Jews, desired of Me."

16 And after we were caught up and transfigured before the throne of God, we were shown all the unspeakable things of the mysteries written by this apostle John[1]; but because of the order which we have received in heaven, we do not report anything, for how much, we ministered among all inhabited earth, and we have recorded the things which we have seen and heard of the revelations written by him, to be revealed, when at last these things begin to occur again between the children of men[2]. [1] **RLDS 3Nephi 13:24-27** / LDS 3Nephi 28:12-15 | [2] **RLDS 3Nephi 13:28** / LDS 3Nephi28:16

17 For how much it is difficult to explain this great mystery which surrounds us, when we ourselves are beginning to understand. The fact is that after a hundred years that have passed since we were removed from our brethren, that is, two hundred and ten years from the time that Christ came among His people, we were considered dead among our kindred, and behold, the Lord brought us back among this people on more than one occasion, for how much there was no more peace and righteousness between them.

18 It was when the people began to divide into classes, and they began to organize churches for themselves, for the purpose of obtaining riches, prestige and glory among their brethren, as I mentioned earlier in this record. Yea, even among those who are remnants of the tribes that each of us was responsible for, who are Jacobites and Josephites and Zoramites.

CHAPTER 4

1 And it came to pass, when we returned among those who are of our people, because they began to be proud, that we ministered among them until the days when Ammoron, the brother of Amos, which were the sons of Amos my brother; yea, the one who replaced my father, Nephi, among the twelve disciples, when he took the leadership of the church among the Nephites.

2 And among them we remain again until the days when Ammoron hid the records that were sacred, three hundred and twenty years after the coming of Christ among the Nephites[1]. It was then, in this year, that the Lord removed us again from the midst of this people[2] and led us to a distant land to minister among the Jews and proselytes Gentiles. Five years after we were taken away again from this people, the Lord appeared to Mormon, when he was fifteen years old, for the purpose of to prepare to obtain these sacred records of the people of Nephi entrusted out to him by this same Ammoron, of whom I spoke earlier. [1] **RLDS 4 Nephi 1:57** / LDS 4 Nephi 1:48 | [2] **RLDS Mormon 1:14-15** / LDS Mormon 1:13-14

3 After some time, being ministering among the Jews and Gentile proselytes both in Jerusalem and in all parts of Asia, we were caught up from that place and reallocated again among this Nephite people. It was when we ministered among our brethren again and in the course these days I began to write this record that we were required to do, and the other two disciples who have accompanied me since then let me write our acts among the people of Christ[1]. — That we should go out on the face of the earth, ministering among all people; yea, among the Gentiles and also among the Jews by virtue of the convincing power of God, who is with us. [1] **RLDS 3Nephi 13:29-30** / LDS 3Nephi 28:18

4 In the course of these years when we, the three disciples, remain among our own people again, behold, we minister to Mormon and his son Moroni[1], for the benefit of the records entrusted to him to compile on plates, for how much these records which I, Jonah, one of the three disciples of the Lord, was commissioned to do, which bears the name "Acts of the Three Nephites[2]" and also of a second record which my father Nephi wrote by request of the Lord as being the book of the "Prophecies of Samuel the Lamanite[3]"; and also the record I mentioned earlier on the "Revelations of John[4]", written by me, Jonah, with aid of the other two disciples, concerning what we have seen and heard when we were caught up. **[1] RLDS Mormon 4:12-15** / LDS Mormon 8:10-12 | **[2] RLDS 3Nephi 13:29-30** / LDS 3Nephi 28:18 | **[3] RLDS 3Nephi 10:34-41** / LDS 3Nephi 23:7-13 | **[4] RLDS Ether 1:113-114; 1Nephi 3:238 -251** / LDS Ether 4:16-17; 1Nephi 14:18-27

5 These records, which I am referring to, were written by me and my father on scrolls of hides, which I delivered into the hands of Mormon at the time we ministered to him and his son Moroni[1], so that Mormon would transcribe them on the plates that were compiling and finally sealing its contents along with other records required by the Lord for a wise future purpose in which we will return and minister together to the one who goes to read these records in the fullness of times. **[1] RLDS Mormon 4:12-15** / LDS Mormon 8:10-12

CHAPTER 5

1 As soon as the twelve began their ministry among the Nephite people, Jesus gave us experiences that can not be described, whose evidence of His love authenticated our ministry wherever we went. If it were not for these special evidences of His love, there would be no reason for these three disciples to want to remain in a world that distills so much hatred and other sentiments derived from Satan; for how much we would suffer every kind of persecution under heaven to take along the pure love of Christ to the most ignored villages around the earth.

2 With the exception of the times we were caught up and reallocated in distant lands, whose language was so different, that most of the time we had to use the gift of tongues to understand what was being said, by whose sense of zeal for the word it was urgent to fill our understanding with the Holy Spirit of God to help us in the different languages to which we were subjected to exhort; and to administer the gospel of repentance among the many nations, tribes, and tongues; without ever letting us down, or being influenced by the opposing sentiments derived from the evil one.

3 It was under such imperative condition, of never to be overwhelmed by the opposing feelings of the devil, which occasionally make up residence in the heart of the natural man, that Jesus warned us to preach and teach the children of men, with the purpose of those who accept our message, coming from the gospel of Christ, to have power in His name to overcome the forces of the enemy in themselves.

4 In view of this, after had passed fourteen years since we were caught up and equipped with these good news, who from the heavens Jesus took me privately among my other two companions, and set me before one of His disciples in Jerusalem, who was about to enter into a debate with the chief apostles of Christ because of the circumcision of the Gentiles, to which I ministered to him not to let the feelings of pride from the evil one take hold of his heart as Jesus foresaw, for how much I have made him realize that true circumcision is the lofty sentiment of Christ in our hearts and that the strange feeling of disagreement was an angel of satan who had moved him for a long time in order to confront the one who held the keys of the high priesthood of the Church in Jerusalem, and this brought tremendous pain to his heart, as if it were a thorn in his flesh.

5 For how much pleaded three times to the Lord to eliminate this evil from his heart, it was that the Lord spoke to him saying: My grace will suffice for you, that is, My Feelings in your heart and behold, My power will be perfected in your weakness for how much you will not exalt yourself to men in the flesh, but will be raised by Me, the Lord, according to the humility that you must obtain, by the ministration of this My servant to thee sent[1]. [1] 2Corinthians 12: 2-9; RLDS 3Nephi 13:25-27 / LDS 3 Nephi 28:13-15

6 When I returned among the Nephites, I joined the other eleven disciples gathered with the Church of Christ from every region around, who sat down to obtain the word of the twelve, and together to share the sacrament, because we taught the people His words, as well as He told us to do. My father Nephi, the main among the twelve, stood before them all and began to speak to the people, saying: We have long waited by the signs announcing the birth of Christ among our brethren in Jerusalem, while the unbelievers tried to nullify our faith by saying that none of this would happen.

7 In later years many of our brothers lost hope and got out of the way. But the promises were real and the prophecies about Christ were fulfilled, one by one before our eyes, until our brethren could clearly discern the time when Jesus would come among us, making us a stronger people in the faith; for the purpose of waiting for the next event until our eyes saw the coming of Jesus Christ, when all could see Him come down from the sky in a beam of light.

8 Let us no longer quarrel in controversy among us, but let us take upon ourselves the commandments of Christ, and stand up in such order, to be united in all things, that together we may overcome any obstacle which Satan may place in our way.

9 Therefore, I want to remind you of these things that were required of us by Jesus Christ, to make us pure in heart, seeking with fidelity to promote good among brothers, without detracting from the words left to us by the prophets of the past, in order that we might obtain the word of God revealed among us, that we may be one, just as He remains united with us through His gospel.

10 These, therefore, are the teachings which Christ left for us, which exist since the beginning, but which were taken from among the people, because they could not endure it, except in the days of Enoch.

11 May we be willing to do the same thing that the Enochians did before the flood now in our present time and let God evaluate our hearts in all things.

CHAPTER 6

1 This is how Jesus told us while He was among us: "If you obey My commandments strictly and keep My covenants, then you will be My special property among all the peoples of the earth. And you yourselves will become a kingdom of priests and a holy nation."

2 As part of His covenant with Abraham, that all the nations of the earth shall be blessed by means of a "chosen seed", He, Jesus, being the "Promised Descendant", kept this same promise among the children of Lehi, placing upon me, Nephi, the presidency of the high priesthood of His Church, and to my descendants after me, from generation to generation as regards that of His administration here in the land of our inheritance, in parallels with the administration of the Church of Christ in the land of Jerusalem; for how much I, and my descendants, according to the diligence that we show for the Gospel of Christ, will be the channels of revelation for the church in this land of promise, since we have no contact with him who holds the keys of the kingdom, laid upon his head by the hands of Jesus Christ when He ministered among the Jews in the land of our ancestors.

3 The basis of this promise, that extended over the firstborn of this seed, it is superimposed upon the head of a righteous descendant from the line of Nephi, if the firstborn has not the desire to fill this office in the place of his father, or is not worthy of such.

4 Being that I, Nephi myself, with whom Christ made this covenant, I tell you with all the strength of my heart, that we, the Nephites, can become, yea, this special property for Jesus Christ among all other peoples from the earth and become a kingdom of priests and a holy nation.

5 Know therefore, all of you, O people of the Church of Christ, that Melchizedek was king and priest at the same time, with office to the high priesthood equal to Enoch. And now we have this same designation left over Nephi's head, and extended to every Nephite nation with the opportunity to produce "a kingdom of priests" and thus, to promote a royal priesthood among the peoples of the earth.

6 But this condition depends on strictly obeying the commandments of Christ and indeed keeping His covenants.

7 Nevertheless, let us definitely understand that the law of Moses, which was brought by our ancestors to this land of promise, has served as a tutor until Christ appears among us and gives us a new covenant, in which the promise made, is that we will be a kingdom of priests according to the order of Melchizedek, in which the high priesthood, as it was in the beginning, shall be restored in the latter days.

8 And now, brethren, behold, I, Nephi, being the one upon whom Christ appointed for presidency of the high priesthood among His Church here in the land of our inheritance, I call you to the general assembly to require you to keep His commandments, and to dignify ourselves before His eyes as a holy people and worthy of His grace.

9 So let us stand up to erect the society and city that Jesus Christ has presented to us, so that we may enter into His rest.

10 Remember, however, that all good feelings come from God; and that evil sentiments proceed from the devil, and that it will not be possible to erect such a United Order, the likeness of the city of Enoch, among the Nephites, if in any way do unbalance to the divine nature that is in you, allowing that the bad feelings derived from evil penetrate into your hearts.

11 Because the devil is an enemy of God and his gifts distill feelings that poison the good heart, waging constant struggle between the gifts of life with those who produce death.

12 Yea, verily, verily, I say unto you; that every feeling that persuades men to do good among their brethren, and impels them to love, it proceeds from the hand of God.

13 But, behold, every sentiment which is opposed to these, though seeming to be beneficial, if it does not meet the needs of its fellowmen, in love, then it proceeds from the evil.

14 Therefore, be careful not to fall into the traps of the devil and be entangled in his fishing net, for the sentiments derived from his gifts tend to be similar to divine feelings, while deceiving the earthly man with such persuasion, to the point of men qualify the bad as good and the good with bad.

15 But, behold, Jesus Christ did not leave us completely forsaken when He departed, but sent us the Holy Spirit, who is given to us by the gift of the Holy Spirit, after baptism, by the laying on of the hands of those who possess the due authority so that we may distinguish good from evil and have a perfect discernment to separate the darkness from the light that fills our hearts, and thus choose to follow the path of clarity through the teachings of His gospel.

16 Therefore, I beseech you, brethren and friends, that together with us remain gathered in the Church of Christ as one body and diligently seek to distinguish between the darkness of the devil and the light of Christ in his way of feeling and put aside all that is detrimental to their way of life.

17 This, therefore, is the secret that God protected and sealed to the knowledge of the past ages, to be revealed only in the fullness of times. Therefore, when He created the first man and the first woman, God endowed them with the fullness of His being and there was no evil feeling in their hearts, but because of their fall, their descendants inherited sin and death, and the weakness of the soul, and the bondage of the spirit in themselves.

18 This causes man to be enslaved by the opposing sentiments created by the arch-enemy of our God, and unless we submit to living under the guidance of heavenly laws, by mutual agreement of the laws of His gospel, we shall never be wholly free from corruption and lusts that continually attack our hearts through a whirlwind of feelings and a stupor of thoughts, which continually divert us from the path we must follow.

19 But with the Holy Spirit of God, through His gifts, Zion will overflow with peace and meekness among the citizens, for the good feelings, as if it were a voice in our ears[1], will have to indicate us the way forward, amen! [1] Isaiah 30:21

20 These were the words of my father, Nephi, in remembrance of the teachings of Christ, when the twelve gathered all the Nephites from among the Jacobites, Josephites, and Zoramites for the purpose of building among them the city of Zion and a new Jerusalem, as prophesied by the prophets of the past. Being that more than a thousand souls were baptized in that occasion because of the words of my father.

CHAPTER 7

1 But behold, Zion, the city whose foundation proceedeth from heaven and expected, by all the prophets that lived before us, shall not come until the words of this book fulfill the prophecies of Isaiah, when then these seals are opened and these words are revealed to the sons of men and by the remnant of Jacob, the Lord God will show in union with the seed of the promise and to every one who will be called by His name in the fullness of times.

2 And thus prophesied Isaiah concerning these days and the chosen seed, through the covenant made with their ancestors: "Behold, the former things already fulfilled, and, behold, now I am announcing unto you new things; and before they occur, I reveal them to you. From the east I will bring his offspring, and in the west I will gather him. I'll tell the north: Deliver them! And to the south: 'Do not hold'; bring My children from afar, and My daughters from the ends of the earth, even every one that is called by My name, and gather in Zion, in the New Jerusalem. And, behold, I will bring forth from them a people who are blind, though they have eyes, and who are deaf, though they have ears, and I will drive them away, because they refuse to see salvation from Me, the Lord, while I gather all the nations into one place."

3 Who among them can announce this and reveal to us the ancient things written in this book? — May he present his witnesses to prove that he is right; so that My people will hear them and say: 'This is true[1]'. [1] Isaiah 43:5-9

4 Therefore, it must be fulfilled in this, that Isaiah's words concerning him who, with stuttering lips and by another tongue, will speak to this people[1], just as it was prophesied by Joseph in Egypt concerning him whom the Lord would call to write these words, but that he will not be able to speak to these people because of his dialect, but that the Lord would summon to minister with him, a spokesman from the loins of Joseph, according to the promises made to our ancestors in relation to the chosen seed in the last days². (1) Isaiah 28:11 | (2) RLDS 2Nephi 2: 32-37 / LDS 2Nephi 3:17-18

5 In these days there will be a transformation of the peoples among whom there will be a pure tongue, for each man and woman will invoke the name of the Lord in their hearts¹, so that the love is the feeling shared by both parties; whether it be between two persons or two groups, or even between different cities, for wherever your people are gathered, there will be the same feelings among brothers. (1) Zephaniah 3:9

6 This project, coming from God, requires first that the people possess the citizenship of Zion in their hearts and this will be the means by which the people of God will show themselves apt and worthy to live in Zion, having a broken heart and a contrite spirit before the Lord.

7 Yea, unless the people united in your feelings begin to build the principles governing Zion in your own hearts, they can never erect a physically structured Zion on earth. This will be impossible unless engraved the laws governing this heavenly home in yourself, and after building yourselves with the spirit, that is, with the pure sentiments that rule Zion, then each of the men and women of God, should extend this same principle, into his own home and so forth through the society of the Church of Christ in general, until all the citizens of Zion are living harmoniously and according to the high standards of the Kingdom of God on earth, just as it is done in the heavens, so that He may come¹. (1) RLDS D&C 65: 1c-1f / LDS D&C 65: 5-6

8 As soon as this becomes a reality, then the spiritual temple, whose living stones, carved and fitting by the words of this book, will be grouped and unified in only one purpose; and only this way will be possible, with unity among all, to build a physical temple in the land, where the Lord will be among His own, as in the days of Enoch and as it came to pass between us, the Nephite people.

9 But these will not be the days when the city of Enoch will come adorned from heaven, like the Heavenly Jerusalem, promised to come down upon the earth, in which the Lord, after gathering His people in Zion and in His stakes in the last days and having prepared the heart of His people to be ready in all things, then after these things coexist in their elect, He shall come and dwell with His people for a thousand years[1]. [1] RLDS D&C 28:2b-2g / LDS D&C 29:8-11

10 Before, however, obey these words and keep the commandments of Christ in your hearts, and teach one another, esteeming each one his neighbor as a brother of blood, while are under these commandments, and subject to the authorities of men; for verily I say unto you, when the Lord cometh into His temple, He shall reveal unto you new commandments[1]. [1] RLDS D&C 38:5a-6a / LDS D&C 38:21-27

11 But as regards this record, whereby the people of the Lord will be ruled in the last days, until He comes to His temple and find a clean people to reveal to them new and great truths[1], behold, we the three Nephites, we will leave written in this record a model, so that the people of the covenant in the last days may have a basis of our society, when among them, this will be revealed. [1] RLDS 2Nephi 12:80; Ether 1:101 / 2Nephi 30:3; Ether 4:7

12 In turn, this people must live in consecration, there being no poor among them, through the covenant of God that will be established among the people, when then, these words will be revealed, for whose promise will never be allowed to be violated, being a people united in purpose and having a pure heart, which will foreshadow the true citizenship of Zion when Christ comes to His temple in the last days[1]. [1] RLDS D&C 42: 8b, 10c / LDS D&C 42: 30, 36

CHAPTER 8

1 The Nephite people, taken then, by their highest sentiments, banished from their midst all resentment that came from the evil one, beginning with sorrow and rancor, then anguish and fear, anger, covetousness and lasciviousness, and many others derived from satan, and whenever an adverse feeling to the heavenly gifts was identified, a record was made of it for the purpose of being worked out at church meetings in general, for the purpose of being replaced by those noble sentiments derived from the bigger Gift, coming from the name of our God, one at a time, until the strife between brethren ceased to exist, and there were no more quarrels among the Nephite people.

2 And, behold, the multitude of those who believed in the words of the disciples of Christ increased, and were baptized into a symbol of a spiritual rebirth, that is, as if buried in the waters of baptism, they abandoned the old sentiments of the evil one, who easily entangled them, in order to be reborn into a new life, clothed with the fullness of the good feelings that are in the name of Christ, which they took upon themselves and were greatly benefited by the gift of the Holy Spirit that was given to them by the laying on of the hands of the twelve; being all of them committed to the gospel of Jesus Christ in order to learn to develop in their fullness in the perfect body that is in communion with the gifts of God, becoming a people united in feelings and understanding as having one heart.

3 For how much was created the most just order, never seen before among brethren, we began to live as an organized church among all the surrounding lands, and my father, Nephi, took upon himself the leadership of the church; having for committee to Lachoneus[1] who had been the supreme judge and governor of the people of Nephi, but who had appointed his son in his place[2], the one who was later murdered in the judge's chair[3], for the purpose of serving God more fully in his ministry, and that symbolically came to represent the right arm of Nephi and, Gidgiddoni[4], who was one of the supreme judges of the people, as his left arm, to which the people had great esteem and consideration[5]. In his place, among the twelve, my father called and ordained to the high priesthood my younger brother, Amos, establishing among us the most sublime and elevated condition that exists in the everlasting gospel, the supreme order of the Church of Christ erected under the foundation of apostles and prophets, which existed before the foundation of the world; with the premise of erecting among this people, the ancient "Order of Enoch", whose foundations among the people of the church of Christ on earth, if done successfully, become the foundations of Zion. [1] **RLDS 3Nephi 2:20-22** / LDS 3Nephi 3:15-17 | [2] **RLDS 3Nephi 3:21** / LDS 3Nephi 6:19 | [3] **RLDS 3Nephi 3:36** / LDS 3Nephi 7:1 | [4] **RLDS 3Nephi 2:24** / LDS 3Nephi 3:19 | [5] **RLDS 3Nephi 3:6-7** / LDS 3Nephi 6:5-6

4 We have always understood that the day would come when we would have to implement this greater law, which was given to Enoch, and later revealed to our ancestors when Moses in the desert clearly taught this same law to the covenant people[1], when he said: that every man Consecrate yourself and your son and his brother, that God may bestow on him a blessing on this day[2]. "But behold there was a dispute between the people, because of their possessions and the gold they had already destined for the Calf of Aaron, for this calf with all its gold was to be thrown out at the command of Moses, but for attachment to this condition corrupted of ambition in their hearts, that same day, were shown to Moses that they were more zealous for the worldly riches than to the sacred covenants established between them and their God." [1] **RLDS D&C 83:4a** / LDS D&C 84:23 | [2] **Exodus 32:29**

5 It was for this reason that the next day Moses said to the people "you have committed a great sin"; and now I will go up to the Lord and I make atonement for your sin. And Moses interceded with the

Lord for the people, saying: O Lord, let not Thy burning anger be risen against this people because of this great sin; for they have made of the spoil which they brought out of Egypt, yea, the gold, in gods for themselves. But now you, O Lord, forgive the sin of this people, if not, exclude me, pray thee, from thy book which thou hast written. And the LORD said unto Moses: "Whosoever shall sin against Me, the same shall I erase out of My book." So now go; lead the people to the place where I told you; behold, My angel shall go before thee; but on the day that I visit, I will visit their sin upon them. And the Lord struck down the people because they worshiped his gold and the golden calf which Aaron made[1]. [1] Exodus 32:30-32

6 And it came to pass in the thirty and sixth year, when all the peoples round about the land were converted, both Nephites and Lamanites, that we started to have all things in common, not existing neither rich nor poor, nor slaves nor free. But they were all partakers of the greater Gift in their hearts, living in communion the fullness of the feelings, united in such a way, that they consecrated all that they possessed for the sake of a greater good — charity.

7 How was this possible? How was it possible that the people lived these precepts without any grumbling or murmuring in relation to their goods being administered by the high council of the church?

8 For all things to take place in order and harmony among all the brethren, the following principles were established among us to be strictly observed by those who wished to live within this Order.

9 It was first necessary to have the desire to be a partaker of this heavenly society, recognizing God as the only Lord over all things, being He a righteous ruler over our properties, whether they were our material resources, our talents, or even our time.

10 Within this principle, it was imperative to recognize that not all brothers would be willing to live under such circumstances. Then the high priests of the sacred order of Melchizedek were established among us, that the law of consecration among the members of the

Church of Christ would be sent to the people, not as a commandment, but only as a principle accompanied with promise, the will of God to all those who feel fit for the call, without there being coercion on the part of the leadership of the church, or resentment toward him who is called to this proceeding, but who rejects him according to the precepts of his heart, due to the designs and the adapted promise of each family's ability to understand or not fully understand the law given us by Christ in order to eliminate the existing inequalities between our brothers and sisters, handing over from our earthly possessions to become stewards of the Lord in regard to His kingdom here on this earth.

11 Therefore, it became necessary to write a record of those who have the desire in their hearts to fulfill this law, and after, to be individually analyzed in relation to the spiritual state and faith of each one to the promises of God and the building of Zion; and all situations concerning the life of each aspirant to join the Order and of his family and of his subsistence, and in common agreement with the applicant, if he stipulate under the consent of his wife and children, his stewardship with the high council.

CHAPTER 9

1 This, therefore, was the statute of the Church of Christ concerning the administration of the law of consecration among its members – Calling each family according to their desires, to determine their stewardship.

2 First, the wealthiest among the people who had their names recorded in the book of those who committed themselves consecrate their possessions to the obtaining of Zion — And being called by name, behold, every one of them was required to make a presentation of his goods, and how much each of them wished to consecrate to the Lord. Since it was not a matter of coercion, it was permitted be a partial consecration of each family, beginning with the tithing required by the law of Moses, and so progressively to the amount that each agreed to give in his heart, without any resentment, as they understood about the Order coming of the Celestial law.

3 Nevertheless, many who began by consecrating only the tithe of all that they possessed and continually giving the tithing of all that they produced; but throughout their lives, passed increasing their consecration, until many did so in their fullness, but each one, in his due time and understanding and giving only the amount which they promised to give; or all they had and produced, or only half of it, or even a third, but were not imposed on them, but all who had the desire to participate were accepted by the Order, according to their yearnings and needs.

4 Thus, the church had resources enough over in its stockpiles, and with that we could call the less well-off to understand their needs and to assist in what was paramount to them.

5 Nevertheless, an assessment was made of the abilities and accomplishments of each individual or family to direct them to a trade, whether among the affairs of the church; of those who were wealthier; or even according to an office that would allow the church to intervene in aid with some commerce or breeding grounds and animal care, or even plantations, for the purpose of this family to get their livelihood, according to the desires of their heart, always having a reserve for the well-being of his family, and the rest returned to the storehouse for consecration for the benefit of others.

6 Therefore was stipulated a period of time, in which this family would receive resources until it was able to support itself with its own stewardship. If this period ended without having reached enough for himself and his family, then the church would make new preparations so that he could obtain the sustenance of his house.

7 This, as some have argued among us, does not fulfill what was required by the Lord Jesus, in having all things in common and in consecrating all that we have and not only a part, retaining the remainder for our own benefit, for how much He said that there would be neither rich nor poor nor slaves nor free among His people.

8 Here is the understanding of the high council, recorded in this statute, concerning the administration of the law of consecration among its members as to the obtaining and administering of their own stewardship. We understand that the law of Christ does not require us to sacrifice everything, it only requires us to live the basic principles of consecration in which we are required that our riches be available to the Lord, and that, while we retain some part of everything we produce in our own warehouses, yet the Lord expects us to be willing, if need be, to sacrifice our houses, lands, and estates, so that there may be a just distribution of riches.

9 This, therefore, is what is really required of us in regard to our stewardship, that there be no rich among us, referring to the "United Order", for how much were some families suffering from need.

10 For verily, verily, I say unto you, unless our intention as a church is to put all in equal conditions, in the sense that there is none among us, having some need, then we shall never be one, as was required us.

11 Wherefore, if there be any rich man among the chosen ones delighting in his goods, while there remaineth a poor man among us, the rich man shall be required to give a portion of all that he hath to the help and benefit of his brother.

12 But if this rich man refuse to help with the possessions he possesses, then he himself will be cut off and expelled from this covenant, but not from the people of the Church, unless his refusal to help is an act of rebellion.

13 Nevertheless, as the Lord is disclosing this great secret to us, the high council of the Church feels sad about the grumbling among you, just as it was in the days of Moses, for how much we can not conceive in our way of thinking, the most effective way to designate this people their portions according to their families, and according to their yearnings and needs, if not by means of a previously arranged order according to the direction of the church of Christ.

14 Without the program of the church to administer your consecrations, there will be no equity among men who will hold their resources for the benefit of their brethren, for how much each one will enter into debate with his neighbor to see who among them should distribute his surplus to the brother in need.

15 Therefore, according to the commandments of Christ, this instrument, the high council of the church, has been instituted to administer all things related to the Order of Enoch, and that the distribution of its resources is just and equitable, without that the wealthy among the covenant people benefit from the sacred order, while others, less fortunate, perish for want of help.

16 This system will provide security and peace among the people of the Lord, for all will be able to worship Him in comfort and harmony, without resentment that some apparently have more than others, for how much a just distribution will be made, according to the desire and the need of each family, so that all may affirm that all goes well in Zion, that all prosper in common accord, and that all are happy within their sphere of stewardship, without there being limit to develop, if the one who received only a portion is willing to rise, as long as there is a responsible administration of the resources of the kingdom of God entrusted to it, delivering three or more times beyond what was required, increasing by personal merit, its own conditions in the family, as long as he maintains his covenant, giving all his surplus to the Church's storehouse.

CHAPTER 10

1 Let us therefore be moved by a higher cause, in which brother watches brother and the Church of Christ as a whole, watch over all the members, so that there is no needy, sick, and afflicted in our midst, that we may show ourselves true disciples of our Lord Jesus Christ, and be worthy representatives of His name amidst a corrupted and misrepresented world.

2 Cease therefore your complaints and your grumblings, for nothing can be more destructive to men in the flesh than to complain continually. Cease looking for mistakes on your brothers or sisters, but love one another just as Christ loved us, for this not only qualifies us to be His disciples, but identifies us as such.

3 Cease to be idle, for this is required of us as servants of a great King, to be vigorous in our affairs, no matter what we are engaged to do with our own hands, doing it with every endeavor of our heart, mind, and soul for the honor and glory of our Lord.

4 Again I must remind you of Christ's commandments about Zion, of loving your wife with all your heart, and only to her you must give exclusive dedication, love, and consideration. And, in turn, she must cling only to thee. And if thou covet thy neighbor's wife, or thy wife if predisposed unto the charms of another man, thou shalt deny the faith, and the Holy Ghost will stay away from this house for how much as sin remains hidden, and if there be no repentance of sinner and subsequently forgiveness by the offended party, then shall be taken out of the midst of the people of Christ.

5 Here is wisdom and a promise; since Zion begins in our own house, then the fundamental bases of the united order of Enoch are the families that compose it. If, therefore, families are weak and disunited in their homes, then the society of Zion will not last for a long time, for when a family falls apart, the foundations of our society are shaken. Nevertheless, if families are not strong and united, then our conception of the Kingdom of God among men on earth will be nothing more than a fable.

6 May purity and goodness be in the mode of speaking between the spouses and practiced in relation to the children, so that their behavior reflects in the outside world, beyond the walls that shelter their homes, developing a society whose language is pure and unblemished to ennoble the magnificence of Zion among the sons of men.

7 If the guidelines of our home are the teachings of Jesus Christ, then we will live in homes where joy reigns, whose branches of our posterity will be firmly rooted in the fruits of the Holy Spirit; love, joy, peace, long-suffering, gentleness, goodness, faith, meekness and temperance; these being the feelings that must fill our earthly abode, as being a heavenly refuge. And, behold, joy is one of its fruits and will overflow through the walls in the homes of Zion.

8 The unity that is required of us as disciples of Christ has no structure if its foundations are not firmly established among the families of Zion. The more united we are to the members of our families, the greater will be the strength of the structures of our unity as God's people.

9 Yea, truly, I tell you, our commitment to make our homes the symbols of Zion, not only prepares us to respond to a higher purpose before the world, but also enables us to live the true unification among brothers, such so that our actions may be perceived out there among the peoples of the Gentile nations, so that we may draw to Christ, all those who have the desire to join us, for the purpose of living Zion in their hearts, in perfect peace and harmony.

10 And it shall come to pass that after you have consecrated your life according to these words, you shall be a steward of the goods of the Lord, to meet the needs of your brethren in the Church according to their deficiencies.

11 Therefore be sober in your stewardship, and put away all the pride and haughtiness that is in your heart, because you will be a representative of Jesus Christ among the children of men.

CHAPTER 11

1 Now, brethren, listen to this premise: We can not think of any more intimate and stronger union than that between God and His Son, the Messiah. The strength of this union was proved by the strict obedience of Jesus up until death. And, by merit obtained by His blood shed for our benefit, He extends to us sinners the invitation to this same sonship with the Father, through adoption; and for this reason, He granted us the glory that God had given him, glory that belongs to sons and daughters, heirs of His Kingdom and therefore, we will no longer be called servants nor servants of His house, but regents and stewards of your property.

2 We are, therefore, members of the family of God, in whom we are required to maintain the unity of spirit in the unifying bond of peace and love from the first day of our existence as a church of Christ, just as I, Jonah, saw with my own eyes, when I was taken from among the Nephites and placed among the apostles in Jerusalem.

3 Where I have learned that there are many Churches of Christ already established in all parts of Israel, and scattered throughout all nations, being all of them Churches of Christ, but who together make up the CHURCH OF CHRIST[1] on the face of the earth; different in customs and tongues, formed by people coming from all the sects of the Gentiles and proselyte Jews who have abandoned their own religious opinions, customs and traditions to give way to this new way of being and feeling in their hearts. [1] Romans 16:16; RLDS D&C 17:25a / LDS D&C 20:81

4 People of entirely different social and cultural backgrounds, just like us, that we were introduced beyond the great waters by our ancestors who came with Lehi and his family to this land of promise, to compose to those other sheep of whom Christ spoke, which He would have to seek also, for the purpose of uniting us into one fold, under the command of one shepherd, having one heart and one soul, and possessing all things in common.

5 Let us therefore abandon all the barriers that divide us and be incorporated into the family of God, stripping us of evil feelings and covering our hearts of the purest and highest gifts from the Holy Spirit, there being no more between us this division between Nephites and Lamanites, nor among Josephites, Jacobites, or Zoramites, but that we are all called by the name of Nephi alone, which has been a symbol of a just and virtuous faith among all these peoples which I have quoted, there being no distinction between the people of the Church, between slave and free, man or woman[1], for we are all one in union with Christ Jesus. [1] Galatians 3:28

6 As for the mediations and portions which you receive in your stewardship, or additions or improvements which you make in the properties which have been assigned to you by the high council, whether dwellings, pastures or plantations, be they animals or any other type of resources from your stewardship, will be designated by the hand of the High Priest that is in charge to keep the storehouses of the Church, and he shall not touch in the things of your consecration without a consensus of the high council, or, by common consent of members of the order at a general assembly of all the stewards who compose it, having these powers equal to that of the highest council for the benefit of some brother or family who have been forgotten by the authorities of the Church. Nevertheless, the order to give the portion due in aid of the needy required by the voice of the people, must come from the one who was appointed and ordained for this blessing, having an evaluation of the situation by the high council, followed by a support of mutual agreement between them.

7 Any portion to be distributed by the Sacred Order must be in accordance with the faith and capacity of the recipient, whose sentiments which form his personality and values that direct his life are not contrary to the stewardship attributed to him. But let your belief in this position be strong enough to keep you steady in your daily business without complaining or weakening.

8 Men are transformed into what they carry within themselves, for this reason will never be truly free, that man whose soul is conformed to be a slave, since he will never behave proudly in spite of his freedom. On the other hand, he who is free in his soul will never be a slave, even if he is kept in captivity, and as soon it must be he is respected by his posture before his masters, because nothing resigns him to this condition.

9 Behold is this being said concerning those who occupy such a post among the Nephites, since there should be no slaves nor free among us, for we are all active stewards in the house of a great Lord. On the other hand, it is not coherent to send away that slave who feels secure in relation to his family and with respect to his affairs and fears in his heart not to know what to do if his freedom is extended to him, since he has spent all his life in the service of his master. To this one must be extended, before freedom, understanding, through a portion between his Lord, or even in some office that does not distance him from his usual duties.

10 On the other hand, it is not fitting for a disciple of Christ to keep under his control one who feels free and master of himself in his heart and who is ready to show his capacity and the inner strength which he has so long hidden within himself.

11 Similarly, each should be assigned a portion commensurate with the values and yearnings they carry in their hearts. For, just as does not feel free that man whose soul conforms to being a slave, similarly a farmer will not know how to correspond to the office of builder, unless there is this longing in his heart.

12 Here are the means of administering each portion and its measures to be assigned according to the stewardships among the members of the United Order of Enoch, so that they are compatible with their abilities or desires and that they conform to their beliefs and values.

CHAPTER 12

1 In concluding these few words that summarize the statute of the Church of Christ in regard to the administration of the law of consecration among its members, I wish to relate a few words by Jesus Christ when He commanded them to be written, to be revealed as new scriptures, according to the time and will of God to the Gentiles in the last days[1]. It was on this occasion that my father, Nephi, brought to Him all the records of our people[2]. [1] RLDS 3Nephi 10:30-33 / LDS 3Nephi 23:4-6 | [2] RLDS 3Nephi 10:35 / LDS 3Nephi 23:8

2 Then it came to pass that Jesus went on to explain all the words that were written in these records to His disciples in particular[1] and commanded my father Nephi to take note of His words to summarize in one single record all things. For behold, their reduced interpretation as regards these records prefigures the covenant people in the last days, when then these prophetic expressions of Jesus are to be revealed to the ranks of faithful men and women who are to compose this United Order to effect the redemption of Zion. [1] RLDS 3Nephi 11:1 /LDS 3Nephi 23:14

3 They will then be eager for the knowledge of these ancient records, written by the Prophets of God in the past, and preserved for a wise purpose in the future, and that, united in one, they will give the elect people in the fullness of times a clear understanding of the way in which we, the Nephites, instituted among our people the Order of Enoch, in the days when we live in peace and harmony among the brethren.

4 May the truths written here by my father Nephi destroy the walls that have always divided society at large and reach out to the poor and the ignorant, making them a wise and learned people in the last days, for how much the rich and the intellectuals among you become the columns of support for the progression of these who will come to the Church of Christ in the last days because of these records, which in turn, will also be preached among all nations, peoples, and languages and make them known among the chosen of the Lord in the fullness of times.

5 Then Jesus said, as He gazed slightly upon the book of Mosiah: "O elect generation, that shall dwell in the limit of the times appointed by My Father, to whom these words shall be trusted, when then it is time to recover My people who are a remnant of the house of Israel, for the last times".

6 Remember the precedents among you, yea, of the days of King Benjamin, that he caused his children to be instructed, that they might become men of understanding, and that they might know of the prophecies which were made by their fathers for the purpose to lead their own children on the path of understanding, and having with them these same directives which King Benjamin had with his little ones.

7 First of all, you should teach your children, just as King Benjamin did with his own children, that these records that now come to you contain the commandments and guidelines necessary for the building of Zion in relation to the last days, and that if it were not because of these plates, which were once sealed, guarded and preserved by My own hand for a wise purpose to be unveiled only in the final part of the fullness of times, then the people of the covenant in the latter days, would remain in ignorance in what it says in respect to the United Order of Enoch.

8 Yea, verily, verily, I say unto you, that if it were not because of these things which were kept and preserved by the hand of the Only Begotten of the Father; yea, I, Jesus Christ, who speaks with you that ye might be able to read and understand the mysteries of God, and have these commandments again before their eyes, then the very fathers, in the fullness of times, would degenerate and they would fall in unbelief, even before their children reached maturity and could never be taught in relation to the things written in this record.

9 But behold, My Father, being the same yesterday, today, and forever, was condescending before the foundation of the world to reveal these things in due time, when it was expedient, that their children might not remain lost in the darkness, but become clear in His ways, when these words are revealed to them.

10 But behold, you are bound as children of the covenant, to live according to all the precepts outlined in this record, dedicated to the preservation and perpetuation of the wisdom revealed in your words, and, above all, engaged in the spread of these of good feelings among your brethren who will be in apostasy in the last days, as it was in the days of the iniquitous king Noah and his priestly class, composed of devout followers, as might be expected of a people blinded by the cunning of the devil, because of the precepts of men and priestly wiles among their leaders, whose priesthood of the Son of God will no longer be active among them, just as He was not active among the covenant people in the days of Alma, when he walked secretly among the people corrupted of the Church of his days and began to teach the words of Abinadi.

11 Yea, Alma was eager to teach all who wished to hear his words, and instructed them secretly, visiting them in their homes, and marking public meetings between the stops of Mormon and baptizing them in their waters in order to live the same principles of the United Order which is now proposed to you, so as to ease the burdens of one another, to weep with those who weep, and to comfort those in need and to be witnesses of these things from God at all times, in wherever you stand, even in front of death, so that you may be found worthy to be numbered among the family of God, and correspond to the pride you must have when you take My name upon you, becoming My authorized representative among men in the flesh.

12 Only in this way can it be recognized by My Father as the true Church established by His Only Begotten Son among men on earth, yea, in the days when I visit them in My temple and again, rename those who repent and come to Me[1], as being the "Church of Christ".

[1] **RLDS D&C 3:16a** / LDS D&C 10: 67

13 Until this day comes, you resume upon you the name that will given by revelation in the introduction of the fullness of times, so that you may be known among the saints which will be scattered throughout, by the name that will be known as My Church in the last days[1]. [1] **RLDS - Revelation on building up Far West (RCH 2:151-152)** / LDS D&C 115: 3

14 For how much, many Churches of Christ[1] will be established by My servants in every corner of the earth, but woe to him who changes the name that will be revealed[2] by Me the Lord. Be it in small things, in the suppression or addition of My word, or in a point of My doctrine, just as I am going to make known at the threshold of the fullness of times. — For it is necessary that every tittle or jot of My revelations be restored to their proper place by My church in the last days until all is fulfilled. [1] **RLDS D&C 98:9d-10c** / LDS D&C 101:67, 75 [2] **RLDS Mosiah 1:17-18** / LDS Mosiah 1:11-12

15 Verily, verily, I say unto you, who dare to change one of these points for Me revealed in the last days, shall be considered as transgressors of My doctrine, as it is written in the book of Mosiah; and if the true Name for Me revealed is altered, even that in the little things I reported, it is because My own doctrine has been altered in their hearts[1], and when this happens, amen to the churches that once were faithful to Me, Jesus Christ. [1] RLDS Mosiah 3:14 / LDS Mosiah 5:11

16 Not at all, they will not be entirely abandoned, but it will serve My interests until I, Jesus Christ, recover what is Mine and restore their inheritance and My name among the people that I will establish in the land that I have appointed them, according to the foreknowledge of God the Father, from the beginning of times.

17 These, therefore, shall be placed in My left hand[1], until God deems it expedient, in due time, to bring them back into their true fold, and to lead them again into His right hand, by observing My commandments, as revealed in these My words, when at last these records are revealed among the covenant people in the last days. [1]

RLDS Mosiah 3:16-17 / LDS Mosiah 5:12-13

18 Behold, a great deal has already been written by your ancestors concerning the authority that should rule My Church on earth, just as you can inquire into the record of Mosiah on Alma, for having received authority from God, he ordained priests, and organized the Church of Christ in his days according to the ancient Order of My Gospel and commanded that they should teach only the things which he himself taught, which were in accordance with the teachings of the holy prophets of the past up to his days, without ever changing what was written earlier.

19 So he told them to preach nothing but repentance and faith in the Lord, lest the confusion of the people of his day be increased further, so it will also occur at the end of times, because of the many interpretations that were and will be rooted in My gospel by the precepts of men, thus stifling My sound doctrine.

20 He also commanded them not to contend among themselves, but to look forward with a single purpose, having one faith and one baptism, done under the proper authority that is in the priesthood, and having hearts intertwined in unity and love one to with others, so as to become legitimate heirs of the Kingdom, and they become children of God.

21 And Alma wisely commanded them to observe the Sabbath day, and to sanctify it, which for the people of the church in the days of Alma was but an act of observing their laws, yea, the laws of Moses. But as regards the last days, as sure as I live, behold, I say unto you, that the forces of the enemy will be manipulating the people of the Lord when these words come unto them, because they no longer observe this commandment in the ambience of their worship.

22 The learned scholars of the law among My people in the last days will be accustomed to look at the Sabbath with contempt, ignoring the fact of what was written by the prophets of the past. And, behold, a genuine repentance will be necessary among the elect of the fullness of times for having in too much profaned the Lord's day.

23 And they will be similar to careless builders, who will begin to erect a temple for Me, the Lord, without regard to the solid foundations by which it must remain unchanged, just as it is the commandment to observe the seventh day.

24 O people of My church, ye with whom My name shall be lifted up, yea, as a standard among the nations in the fullness of times, once and for all, you should understand that the relationship between the seventh day and the people of God is at the core of the whole truth of My gospel from before the foundation of the world until its end, and that it is perpetually intertwined with the sacrament of holy supper that I instituted among My apostles before I left Jerusalem.

25 Except in new moon, for how much the sacrament is to be offered at the end of the day, when the first moon appears in the heaven of every month, every month of the year, on any day of the week, as a special day of adoration[1]; yea, on this day My people will hold a special banquet[2]; in regard to the newly baptized members of My Church, so that, they can for the first time share My body which has been given for the benefit of their sins in the flesh and of My blood for the sake of an everlasting life, just as it was done among My disciples and the Nephite people, so that on this new moon day you must be filled by the Holy Spirit in a true spiritual banquet[3] in honor of those who repent and are baptized in My name[4]. [1] Ezekiel 46:1-8 | [2] 1Samuel 20:5,18,24,27,34 | [3] RLDS 3Nephi 8:31,38 / LDS 3Nephi 18:4,9 | [4] RLDS 3Nephi 8:38-43 / LDS 3Nephi 18:9-12

26 For as, the first moon, they shine for the first time among My people on earth, for how much My angels celebrate with this first communion between them and the heavens, among whom many hear their songs of praise in the land.

27 Behold, it is on the seventh day, which was sanctified by My Father, that should introduce yourself as people before God, and offer unto Him your sacraments, just as they are revealed in the holy scriptures, in righteousness of heart and a contrite spirit[1]; so that you may keep yourselves clean from one Sabbath to another, and as Alma has asserted among you, may render thanks to the Lord your God every day. [1] RLDS D&C 59:2e-2f / LDS D&C 59: 8-9

28 These, therefore, are two indivisible signs of My priesthood, which in all ages Satan has annulled for the purpose of inhibiting the full force of My power among My people, for it is in the observance of the Sabbath law and the correct practice of the sacramental ordinance that manifests the power of divinity among the sons of men in the flesh[1], and if these are not observed exactly as stipulated by Me and My Father, even before the foundation of the World, to be the same from everlasting to everlasting[2], without that there be change in any letter or point of My doctrine, just as the eternal priesthood, which is without beginning or end of days, can not be altered, so it is with the My words which I have commanded you. [1] RLDS D&C 83:3c / LDS 84:20-21 | [2] Psalms 90: 2

29 Behold, verily, verily, I say unto you, O ye elect people in the fullness of times, even as I say to these My Nephite disciples, that you will examine these things; and I say unto you also, and verily I

command you that ye should search these things diligently according to the words of Isaiah. For he not only spoke all things concerning the people of Israel, but also made an account of the things that are to be restored among the Gentiles in regard to the fullness of times, that from one new moon to another and from one sabbath to another shall all flesh come to worship before Me, the Lord[1]. [1] Isaiah 66:23

30 And all the things that Isaiah said were and will be fulfilled according to the things that he wrote. Therefore hearken thou to My words; and that My disciple, Nephi, write the things which I have spoken unto you concerning My people in the latter days; and according to the time and the will of the Father, these things will come to your knowledge.

31 And whosoever shall hearken unto these words of mine and repent and be baptized shall be saved. Therefore examine what the prophets concerning the Sabbath have said, for many bear witness to these things, as Isaiah testified, when he spoke of the full restoration of the observance in the dispensation of the fullness of times, when saying: Thus saith Jehovah: "Take heed to judgment, and do that which is just, for, behold, My salvation is about to come, and My righteousness to be revealed. Blessed is the man that doeth this, and the son of man that shall keep to this commandment – "To keep the Sabbath, and not to profane it[1]". [1] Isaiah 56:1-2

32 These words, therefore, apply to the Gentiles in the last days. Yea, to whom this record is to be revealed in the fullness of times, to redeem My people, which is a remnant of Jacob, as Isaiah foretold when he wrote: "Thus saith the Lord GOD, which gathereth the dispersed of Israel, and lo, I will yet gather others unto him[1]." [1] Isaiah 56:8

33 Therefore, I preserve this doctrine and preserve it by My own hand to be restored in the last days for the purpose of fulfilling the words of Isaiah concerning the day on which I, Jesus Christ, will definitely seal the law and the testimony through these ancient Records for the restoration of this important commandment among My disciples that I will gather with the house of Jacob[1]. [(1)] Isaiah 8:16-18

34 And once again I will recite to you the words of Isaiah concerning this people who await Me in the fullness of times: "And they that shall proceed from thee shall build the ancient ruins; and thou shalt raise up the foundations of many generations; and thou shalt be called the repairer of the breach, and restorer of the ways of our inheritance."

35 If therefore thou turn aside thy foot from profaning the Sabbath, and to take care of thy own interests on My holy day; if you call the Sabbath a delightful and holy day of the Lord, honorable, and honor it not by following your own ways and not intending to do your own will or speaking empty words on this day, then you will delight in the Lord your God.

36 And I Myself will cause you to ride upon the high places of the earth of your inheritance, and I will uphold thee as the heirs of Jacob thy father: for the mouth of the Lord hath said, that ye are a remnant of his seed[1]. [(1)] Isaiah 58:12-14

CHAPTER 13

1 Therefore, Alma also commanded that the priests whom he had ordained should work with their own hands for their sustenance, except the evangelists, establishing themselves among them one day of each week, besides the Sabbath, in which they were to meet to teach the people and worship the Lord their God; and should they also meet as often possible.

2 And then, so that the words of Mosiah may serve as a reference to My people in the fullness of times, the book of Mosiah makes it clear that Alma began the Order of Enoch again among the people of the Church of Christ in his day, when he commanded that his members should share their goods, each according to your possessions; he who had abundantly, should share more abundantly in reason of him who had little; and whoever had nothing, to him would be given. And so, according to their free will and because of their good feelings, they should share their goods with needy priests, yea, and with every needy and naked soul.

3 And this, he told them, by order of God[1]; because he received revelation from Him, and so they walked right before God by listening to their prophet, helping one another, both materially and spiritually, according to their needs. [1] RLDS Mosiah 9:63 / RLDS Mosiah 18:29

4 And it came to pass after some time that Alma and his people were driven into the wilderness, as My people in the fullness of times shall also be driven into the wilderness - where God the Father shall prove the quality of their faith in these words, for the purpose of transforming, purifying, and preparing them for the attainment of their inheritance with Me, Jesus Christ.

5 But after eight days run away in the wilderness they came to a very beautiful and pleasant land, a land of pure waters, which had been prepared beforehand to receive them, and as soon as they had arrived in this land and pitched their tents, and they began immediately to cultivate the soil and to build buildings; in being an industrious and hard working people.

6 And being a free people, he established himself among them, that they would not have for leader or minister, men who were not God-fearing; but that they should walk in His ways, and keep His commandments.

7 To the people of the Church, Alma taught that each one should love one's neighbor as oneself, so that there would be no intrigues between them. And so Alma, being the High Priest of My sacred Order[1], became the founder of the Church among them, appointing

authorities to preach and teach the people of the Church, so that there would not be among the candidates for evangelizers, those who were not authorized by God to teach, being that all members, men and women, were appointed to speak in congregational meetings, with the purpose of priests preparing them for ministerial work in the preaching of the gospel. [1] RLDS Mosiah 11:17 / LDS Mosiah 23:16

8 And so as iron sharpens iron[1], so My people become more and more qualified in the art of teaching and skilled in the handling of the words, in order to offer the offers of his lips[2] as sacrifices to God in the preaching of this Gospel to the world, because all are partakers of the body of the Church, by whose sacrifice offered with words and songs of praise are more pleasing to Me than a bull on the altar[3].

[1] Proverbs 27:17 | [2] Hosea 14:2 | [3] Psalms 69:30-31

9 And it came to pass that no one was given authority to preach or teach, except by the call of God, through Alma. He therefore consecrated all the priests and all the evangelizers; and no one was consecrated unless he was righteous, who watched over his people and edified them with things pertaining to the righteousness and the good feelings of the Gospel of Christ.

10 And it came to pass that they began to prosper much in this new land; where they multiplied and prospered greatly. Nevertheless, the Lord deems it convenient, from time to time to prove His people; yea, He proves his patience and his faith after making them prosper abundantly. But he who trusts in Him shall be lifted up at the last day.

11 And so it was with the people of Alma as to the time when they became captives of the Lamanites and of Amulon, until the day when the people of the church ceased to cry out with their voices, but "opened their hearts" before the altar of God, invoking Him in their feelings and acknowledging that no one could save them except the Lord their God; yea, the God of Abraham of Isaac and of Jacob.

12 And it came to pass after God had made them free and showed them His great power; that it was possible for them to return to the land of Zarahemla and Abundance, as it shall be with My people in the fullness of times, when at last they shall return to the land of their inheritance after having passed through the wilderness and take possession of a far country that I will prepare for them beforehand through My chosen ones in the last days, and if it were not for the sake of My chosen ones[1], none of them would be saved to preserve them from the sudden destruction that will come upon all in their homeland. And just as it happened to Alma and his people while they were in the wilderness, they will be cleansed from the condition of their hearts, the day they learn to invoke Me with a broken heart and a contrite feeling. [1] Matthew 24:20 IV

13 And behold, God did not give you a spirit of bondage, but of adoption, that you may be of good courage to rise to a spiritual condition that is above the feelings which enslave men in this captive state proposed by Satan, and walk in the certainty that you are a child of God, who has been placed in your hearts through the feeling of filiation given by the laying on of hands, the Gift of the Holy Spirit, in which you can call in your heart the "Father of our spirits[1]" in a way that He actually listens and answers your prayer, extending His powerful hand to help you. [1] Romans 8:12-15; Galatians 4:6-9

14 For verily, verily, I say unto you these last words concerning the book of Mosiah, as regards My people when this record is revealed unto them, that the feelings derived from a broken heart before My Father are the greatest power that is in the world; for only a sincere heart, moved by a contrite feeling, is able to move the hand of Him who rules the whole universe.

15 Yea, verily I say unto you, that it is in the pure and lofty sentiments proceeding from the gifts of God that all wisdom from the heavens is hidden; because they contain within themselves the possibility of sensitizing the feelings of the one who is All-Seeing and, through sincerity and truthfulness of urgency, moves heaven and earth to the aid of that son who truly knows how to speak with the Father.

16 However, the Father will do nothing for His children on earth, for how much as there is a possibility of them doing something for themselves. Remember therefore these words of mine, which again come to you through this record, to observe carefully the birds of the heaven, for they do not reap nor store in barns, but the Father who is in heaven feeds them, day after day.

17 On the other hand, if you look closely at the birds of the heaven, as you are required in this parable, you will see that though they do not reap nor store in barns their grains; they have to leave of their nests every day looking for food in order to get them by their own efforts. In this, therefore, is manifested the Divine wisdom of which I have spoken, in which birds, as well as the children of men, obtains the promise that the Father will nourish them, for He will never let anything be lacking for His sons, for how much they believe in themselves.

18 This, then, is an act of faith, and serves all matters under heaven, because faith precedes action, being dead in itself if it does not produce some attitude. This is the foundation of the wisdom and the lofty sentiments that move the people of the covenant to excellent works, because it has this promise of My own voice, that the Father will be with His people, to protect and to assist them, when then there is nothing else you can do for yourself, Amen.

19 Just as it was said to My disciples, I tell this generation about which I prophesy at this moment that the mysteries of God[1] are given in these words of mine, for this the words of this book reveals that the essence of the gifts from My Father are the pure feelings that lodge in your hearts. [1] Matthew 13:8-16 –IV

20 Therefore, guard your hearts from the evil feelings which proceed from the devil, which suddenly are played like poisoned darts of all sorts of lasciviousness, wrath and anger; and which penetrate your hearts and inflame even the saints of God with the evil feelings coming from him, the evil being, with the purpose of obstructing the work of the Father in bringing salvation to the sons on earth.

CHAPTER 14

1 And taking the book of Jacob into His hands, Jesus proceeded to say: This is why the scriptures of the ancient prophets speak by means of illustrations, so that, seeing no one notices and does not pay attention to his message. For it is necessary that this simple truth related to your feelings remain as a sacred secret, from generation to generation, so that only in the final part of the fullness of times this may come in its purity and perfection, without ever having been distorted under the precepts of men.

2 Happy, therefore, are your eyes, for they watch, and your ears, for they hear the reading of these words of mine and unravel this great mystery that was hidden by all the times predetermined by Me and My Father, since before the foundation of the the world, to be revealed to My humble followers, only when the workers of My vineyard are ready to do the work in the field abandoned by the earliest workers, for the purpose of restoring the gifts of God proceeding from His Name among those who take upon themselves the name of His Only Begotten Son, Jesus Christ, and receives the 'Gift of the Holy Spirit'.

3 And thus you may recognize the true sentiments of My priesthood and My grace among the children of men as to the gifts of the evil that were created by Satan to deceive and overcome the heavenly gifts in the world of mankind.

4 Listen, therefore, to him who has the desire to understand even more this great mystery, which is revealed to you in this moment in which My words come to you in the last days. For verily I, Jesus Christ, make known to you the meaning of the parable of the good olive tree prophesied to the house of Israel, now that you can understand in its simplicity this analogy uttered by My servant Zenos with regard to good feelings from God to His children on earth.

5 Behold, the olive tree symbolically represents the people of God from the beginning of times, for it grows and produces fruit even on soils with little water, and even though if cut at the foot of its trunk, it has the vitality to regenerate itself again from of its roots. And although an olive tree is immersed for many days under the waters of a flood, it tends to survive and after lowering the waters, continues to produce fruits in abundance as if nothing had suffocated its branches. Remember that it was a leaf of an olive tree that the dove brought to Noah at the end of the flood.

6 And if it were not enough all their resistance to survive in critical and adverse situations, when grafted branches of a grafted olive tree into a good olive tree, it is able to make them into good olive trees again, so that they are replanted, as branches of good olives again.

7 For this reason, I and My Father compared the house of Israel to all those who make up the Church of the Lamb to a good and leafy olive tree, which the Lord of the vineyard planted next to water currents, for the purpose of producing fruits according to its season; and whose leaves would never wither[1]. [1] Psalms 1:3

8 And now, to what shall I compare these water currents? To the good feelings derived from the Gift of God, which flows along with the other sentiments derived from the love of God among the covenant people that persists in observing My commandments.

9 But as it is written in the dream of My servant Lehi, these waters came from a spring near the tree of life[1], where the people of God must arrive and delight with their fruits, provided they remain firmly grasped to the rod of iron which will lead them, according to the words of Nephi, unto the fountains of living waters; that is, to the tree of life from which it proceeds its water source, which are symbols of the love of God[2]; yea, from this Greater Gift of which I have spoken to you, whence proceed all the good sentiments of My gospel. [1] RLDS 1Nephi 2:54-56 / LDS 1Nephi 8:13-14 | [2] RLDS 1Nephi3:68-69 / LDS 1Nephi 11:25

10 Nevertheless, the roots of the good olive tree, which is the house of Israel, stretched under the slopes of the river, where its waters were already mingled with impurity, symbolically representing the sentiments created by Satan, by whose priestly wiles he cast his gifts just below the source of God's gifts, and he came to defile His leafy olive tree, so that his roots, strewn on the slope of this river of filthy waters seen by Lehi[1], began to absorb the impurities from the evil one, and its fruits, which are the feelings of the people who make up the house of Israel, because they were so distracted by other things, did not perceive the filth of the water that absorbed the seed in their hearts, as being the depths of hell[2], to involve them in the senses, and thus the good olive tree grew and grew in its field, that is, among the nations of the world. [1] RLDS 1Nephi 4:43-45 / LDS 1Nephi 15:26-27 | [2] RLDS 1Nephi 3:124 / LDS 1Nephi 12:16

11 The original olive tree, therefore, had grown old in its customs and traditions, and even though the streams of dirty water were mixed with clean waters, that is to say, feelings of all kinds, coming from both sides, its roots were fed in such a way that its dirt appears in the fruits and also in its trunk, just above the earth, which prefigures the human heart; and thus, the sap of its essence was lost, because of these precepts of the enemy, as being a plague infesting its inner structure.

12 But behold, the Lord of the vineyard saw that His olive tree was beginning to wither, and so He cut down all his wild branches, yea, the people who affected the people of Israel with their feelings contaminated by the filth of Satan and his grumbling infecting all the nation of Israel in the days of Moses.

13 When then they were in the wilderness of their afflictions, and God took from the midst of His people the wild branches, thus pruning His good olive tree and digging about so that the good water, coming from its clear spring, descended to its roots again, so as to make their fruits pure and desirable for themselves, and began to care for them in the hope of sprouting new and tender branches so that they produce good fruit in the next season, that is, new people in the next generation, and so it was, according to your words[1]. [1]

RLDS Jacob 3:30-32 / LDS Jacob 5:1-4

14 And after much time had passed, small and new branches began to sprout, who were the lesser prophets that arose between the nation of Israel and those who listened to His words and the law of Moses.

15 But, behold, his feelings were still tender, while the canopy of the olive, which foreshadowed the nation's leaders in their entirety, was dying, in the sense that none of the priests were pure enough to the Lord of the vineyard, languishing the highest part of the good olive tree. Then the owner of the vineyard said to His servant that it is painful to think that this dedicated generation of new branches, which is still tender, while the canopy of My olive tree perishes and will not have strength in itself to keep My fruits in the good olive tree that I took care of so much, all these days[1]. [1] RLDS Jacob 3:34 / LDS Jacob 5:6

16 It happened then that the Babylonians came, like branches of a wild olive tree to be grafted among the nation of Israel, for how much the main branches that were beginning to dry up were destroyed by the fire when the King of Babylon took captive many of the new and tender branches in order to graft them, according to the words of the Lord of the vineyard; "and I will graft them whithersoever I will;" for though the nation of Babylon will perish, as it were prophesied, the owner of the vineyard should preserve its fruit from the mixture of races that would occur between the Jews and the Gentiles. Therefore they were captives of this nation to fulfill the purpose of the Lord of the vineyard, to take from among the nations of the earth some new and tender branches of the house of Jacob, and to graft them where it should be. [1] RLDS Jacob 3:35-42 / LDS Jacob 5:7-10

17 And it came to pass in the days of those kings that Daniel, the Servant of the Lord, became master of the magicians-astrologers[1] from the east, and came to teach his princes and noble confederates and vassals, among whom were many Jews, which have passed their knowledge for your children, spreading from generation to generation their knowledge of astrology even among the many synagogues that were erected in the land of the East, when then the Lord of the vineyard went to hide the natural branches of the good olive tree in the nethermost parts of the vineyard, some in one part, others in another, spreading these apprentices of the wisdom of Daniel the prophet according to His pleasure and will[2]. [1] Daniel 1:20; 4:9 | [2] RLDS Jacob 3:48 / LDS Jacob 5:14

18 And it came to pass that a long time went by, and the Lord of the vineyard said unto His servant, come, let us go to the vineyard to work on it. And it came to pass that the Lord of the vineyard, and also the servant, went down into the vineyard to work[1]. It was when the words of Isaiah, both recited and researched in the East, were fulfilled through teaching propagated by Belteshazzar in the wisdom schools of Babylon, where they studied the scriptures with all peoples in relation to the "future descendant"; and up until even among the instructed rabbis of the Hebrew people in their respective synagogues, in the distant lands of Israel. [1] RLDS Jacob 3:49-51 / LDS Jacob 5:15-16

19 Which had been grafted into the wild olive tree, and for this reason, they learned to map the heavens, so that they could identify that star that had been foretold by the prophets that does not belong to the starry skies, for how much its manifestation in the night sky would foreshadow the birth of the 'promised descendant' among men on earth.

20 These, then, were the natural branches of the good olive tree in a foreign land, and so did those branches of the olive tree that were brought and grafted into the good olive tree; all have borne fruit in their respective station, and have mingled together.

21 And after a long time, a child is born in the land of Jerusalem, as prophesied by the ancient prophets, in the city of Bethlehem[1]; and the people that walked in darkness saw a great light; and they that dwell in the land of the shadow of death, yea, in the land of the east, the light of the morning shone upon them, proclaiming the coming of Him that would be called by the name of Wonderful, Counselor, the Mighty God, the Everlasting Father, Prince of Peace[2]. [1] Micah 5:2 | [2] Isaiah 9: 6

22 And guided by this light was that the astrologers of the orient took the way to the land of Israel, where the throne of David is set as it prophesied, in search of the land of Naphtali, in the way of the Jordan, Galilee of the nations[1]. [1] Isaiah 9:1-2, 6-7

23 Then the fruits of the branches that came out of the wild olive tree, and were attentive to the signs of every season, whose branches were scattered throughout the region of the east, and the Lord of the vineyard saw that they were good branches; and its fruits, that is, the sentiments of the Jews born in the East and educated in the synagogues of that region, according to the teachings of the prophets, were similar to the fruits of the Jews of the land of Israel, that is, the natural feelings[1]. [1] RLDS Jacob 3:52-53 / LDS Jacob 5:17

24 For this reason they were easy to mix among their brethren in the land of their ancestors, for they absorbed the moisture of its root, so that its root produced much strength; and because of the great strength of the root the grafted branches produced good fruits, so that they could be grafted again into the good olive tree, that is, that could mix without being aware of the difference between one and the other[1]. [1] RLDS Jacob 3:54-57 / LDS Jacob 5:18

25 And it came to pass that the servant said unto his master: How art thou come to plant here this tree, or this branch of the tree? For behold, the East was the lowest and unproductive part of all the land of your vineyard. And the Lord of the vineyard said unto him: Give Me no counsel. I knew it was an unproductive piece of land; so I told you that I have treated this first tree all this time; and you see that it produced many fruits; gather them, therefore, and keep them for the proper season, that I may bring them unto me[1]. [1] RLDS Jacob 3:63-66 / LDS Jacob 5:21-23

26 And it came to pass that the Lord of the vineyard said unto His servant, Look here; see that I have also planted another branch, yea, a second branch in the tree of this unproductive land of the east; and you know that this piece of land was more unproductive than the first. But look at the tree. Behold, I have dealt with her all this time, and she bore many fruits; gather them also, and keep them for a due season, that I may preserve them for Myself.

27 And it came to pass that the Lord of the vineyard spake again unto His servant, Look here, and see another branch which I have planted; yea, a third of the orient, and, behold, I have dealt with him also and brought forth good fruit, and of these three branches I will bring those who will serve Me[1]. [1] RLDS Jacob 3:65-67 / LDS Jacob 5:23-24

28 And from these three productive branches, coming from the unproductive land from which the Lord of the vineyard mentioned to His servant, came Jews from the schools that map the stars, in order to accompany the development of this boy who was born in Bethlehem, in the land of Jerusalem.

29 Being the first of these three, Bunai, noble Rabbi over the synagogues of Greece, which caused him to be accepted into the sect of the Pharisees in Jerusalem, where he had established his residence

from My birth until the days of My resurrection, and among the natural Jews of the good olive tree he mixed with the name of Nicodemus. The second known as Joseph; Jewish born in Rome and appointed magistrate in the land of Judea; with powers derived from a judge over the city of Arimathea, which was situated three hours northwest of Jerusalem, where he was a member of the Sanhedrin, but My particular disciple[1]. The third, noble merchant of the region of Antioch, he preferred to stay away from the leaven of the Pharisees in Bethany under the name Lazarus. [1] **John 19:38-40**

30 These were the three branches from the wild olive tree planted in the lowlands of the orient; and were great friends from the beginning to the end of My journey on the Earth of their ancestors.

31 And the Lord of the vineyard said to the servant, Look here and see the last, behold, it refers to the descendants of Lehi, the branches of the original olive tree planted in the land of his inheritance. Behold, I have planted them on a piece of fertile land; yea, in this land overseas, and I took care of it all this time, and only a part of the tree bore good fruit; but the other part of the tree produced bitter fruit; and it happened that a long time passed since I planted them and the branches did not produce good fruit[1]. And the Lord of the vineyard saith unto His servant: come, let us go down, and let us return to work in this vineyard. For behold, the time draweth nigh, and the end shall come soon; therefore, I must save fruit for Myself, for the next season[2]. [1] **RLDS Jacob 3:68** / LDS Jacob 5:26 | [2] **RLDS Jacob 3:70-73** / LDS Jacob 5:27-29

32 It so happened after the third day after I was resurrected in Jerusalem, that I came to be among My other sheep of whom I have spoken, that these I would also have to visit, which are a branch of the house of Israel planted in a fertile land. But behold, I say to you, that although they live a period of total harmony for a short time, with the noble sentiments coming from the Most Great Gift from the Spirit of God; behold, in the course of his future days the natural tree, that is, the Jews into whom the branches wild, which are the Gentiles that were grafted, will be overburdened with every kind of fruit, both of Jew and Gentile, and this will occur both in the land of your ancestors, as well as in this land of your inheritance[1], for how much, many shall come from other lands, even many Jews, from various tribes of Israel, and also from Ephraim. But, behold, there shall be many Gentiles coming from afar, from places overseas, and it shall be seen that none of their fruit shall be good unto Me in this period of time[2]. **[1] RLDS Jacob 3:74** / LDS Jacob 5:30 | **[2] RLDS Jacob 3:78** / LDS Jacob 5:3

33 It is therefore at this time that the prophecies concerning the days of that predicted darkness are fulfilled, which will cover the earth, when the sun will set on the prophets[1], and the light of men will become darkness[2] and there will be no one to tell you how much longer this will last[3], by what form is that church that was foretold to Nephi, son of Lehi, that would be the most abominable of all the churches, whose founder is the devil, and who, for the praise of the world, will destroy the saints of God and also enslave them in that land that separates the seed of Lehi, through the many waters[4]. **[1] Micah 3:6** | **[2] Jeremiah 13:16** | **[3] Psalms 74:9** | **[4] RLDS 1Nephi 3:140-145** / LDS 1Nephi 13:5-10

34 And the Lord of the vineyard said unto the servant, What shall we do for this tree, that it may again store its good fruit for Me? And the servant said to his master, "Look, because you have grafted branches of the wild olive tree, that is, the Gentiles in the natural olive tree, through Christ, then they nourished the roots, so that they are alive and not dead; see, therefore, that they are still good".

35 But, behold, the Lord of the vineyard said unto His servant: It is of no use to Me the tree and its roots if they bear evil fruit. Nevertheless, knowing that their roots are good I will preserve them for a future purpose; and because of their great strength they have produced good fruits of the grafted branches, and henceforth the grafted branches will grow and overcome the roots of the tree; and because the branches are grafted will grow and overcome the roots, then it will produce many evil fruits and be thrown into the fire, unless we do something to preserve it[1]. **(1) RLDS Jacob 3:79-84** / LDS Jacob 5:33-37

36 And it came to pass that the Lord of the vineyard saith unto His servant: Let us go down into the lower parts of the vineyard, to see whether the natural branches also produced forth evil fruit. And it came to pass that they saw that the fruits of the natural branches were corrupted also because of that abominable church; yea, the first and the second, and also the last; and all the churches that had tried to bring forth good fruit had been corrupted[1]. But, behold, the Lord of the vineyard then said to His servant, this is the fulfillment of the vision of Nephi concerning that man whom he saw that was separated from the seed of his brethren by the many waters; and I saw that the Spirit of God came down and inspired the man; and as the man went through the many waters, he came to the seed of his brethren which was in the land of the promise, just as he saw the Spirit of God inspire other Gentiles, which are branches of the wild olive tree, and therefore remnant of the house of Israel; and they went forth out of the captivity, and crossed over the many waters, and received the good land by inheritance, for they humbled themselves before the Lord; and the power of the Lord was with them[2]. **(1) RLDS Jacob 3:86-87** / LDS Jacob 5:39 | **(2) RLDS 1Nephi 3:147-151** / LDS 1Nephi 13:12-15

37 But these last grafted branches, that is, Gentiles brought to this land overseas, will also surmount the seed of Lehi and his brethren and the branch of the seed of his brethren will dry up and die; and the Lord will cry for his loss, because all the fruit of His vineyard will perish except these; but now are also corrupted, and all the trees of His vineyard are of no avail except to be cut down and cast into the fire[1]. **(1) RLDS Jacob 3:88-92** / LDS Jacob 5:40-42

38 But, behold, the Lord of the vineyard cut off the trees that obstructed this piece of land, and planted another tree in his place[1], fulfilling the promise which Joseph the son of Jacob had obtained from God the Father, when He told him that He would raise from his loins a "fair branch" to the house of Israel; and being righteous, though he is Gentile, will be counted as being part of the natural olive tree; for he will be truly a descendant of Joseph; not the Messiah, but that "graft" of which Lehi prophesied, which is to come in the fullness of the Gentiles in the last days, when your descendants have degenerated, fallen into unbelief, yea, for the space of many years and for many generations after the Messiah manifests himself in person to the children of men, then the fullness of My gospel shall come to the Gentiles; and of the Gentiles, to the remnant of your descendants[2]. [1] RLDS Jacob 3:94 / LDS Jacob 5:44 | [2] RLDS 1Nephi 4:16 / RLDS 1Nephi 15:13

39 Yea, to bring the Gentiles out of the darkness, which shall be upon the earth in those days; nevertheless, this graft will be a seer who will guide My people again to the path of light[1]. [1] RLDS 2Nephi 2:6-10 / LDS 2Nephi 3:5-6

40 And the Lord of the vineyard saw that a part of this planted tree in the last days, produced good and bad fruit, that is, good and bad feelings in the people who make up the branches of His vineyard; in such a way that the brave branch produced bad fruits that surpassed the good branch[1]. And now, after all the care we have taken with the vineyard, its grafts have become corrupted, so that none of them bring forth good fruit; and these I hoped to keep in order to get its fruits for Me, for the season to come. [1] RLDS Jacob 3:95-96 / LDS Jacob 5:45

41 But, behold, "they" became like the wild olive tree, and they are of no use except to be cut down and cast into the fire; but I feel sorry to lose them just like the rest of My vineyard. — What else could, however, I have done in My vineyard? I have nourished them, and I have digged about them, and I have pruned, and I have fertilized its roots; and I have stretched forth mine hand almost all the days long; but behold, the end draweth nigh, and therefore I feel I have to cut down all the trees of My vineyard, and cast them into the fire, that they may be burned. Who is it that has corrupted My vineyard[1]? [(1)]

RLDS Jacob 3:97-104 / LDS Jacob 5:46-47

42 And it came to pass that the Lord of the vineyard said unto the servant: Let us go, and hew down the trees of the vineyard, and cast them into the fire, that they shall not cumber the ground of My vineyard; for I have done all I could. What could I have done more for My vineyard? — But behold, the servant said unto the Lord of the vineyard, Spare it a little longer. And the Lord said: Yea, I will spare it a little longer; for it grieveth Me that I should lose the trees of My vineyard[1]. [(1)] **RLDS Jacob 3:109-111** / LDS Jacob 5:49-51

43 Let us therefore take the branches of these which I have planted in the low parts of My vineyard, and graft them on the tree from which they proceeded, that is, in the original graft; and pluck from the tree the branches that give the most bitter fruits and graft in its place the natural branches, coming from the original tree, so that the tree does not die, but preserve for Me your roots, to comply with My purpose.

44 And, behold, the roots of the natural branches of the tree, which I planted where I pleased, are still alive; scattered throughout all the land of My vineyard, that I may preserve them also for a purpose of mine. I will therefore take its branches and graft them again into the original tree. Yea, I will graft upon them the branches of the original tree, that I also may preserve the roots unto Myself, that when they are strong enough they may bring forth good fruits for Me, and I may have glory in the fruit of My vineyard[1]. [(1)] **RLDS Jacob 3:112-117** / LDS Jacob 5:52-54

45 And it came to pass that they took of the natural tree, which had become wild, and grafted in the natural trees, which also had become wild. And they also took from the natural trees, which had become wild, and grafted in their original tree, that is, though they were many wild branches, all shared in common the sap of the original tree, so that the Lord of the vineyard said to the servant; do not pluck the branches out of the trees, except those that are very bitter; and you shall graft in them as I say[1]. [1] **RLDS Jacob 3:118-120** / LDS Jacob 5:55-57

46 And the Lord of the vineyard then said to His servant not to pluck out these wild branches, which were scattered throughout all the vineyard. Thus, He said, we will "take care again" of these trees[1], to fulfill that which was written by Nephi concerning the Lord of the vineyard, when He shall stretch forth His hand a second time, to recover His people, which is of the house of Israel[2], for the purpose of "swapping the branches," that is, grafting the natural branches in their original tree, so that the Lord of the vineyard came to rejoice for having preserved the roots and also the branches of the first fruit[3]. [1] **RLDS Jacob 3:112-117** / LDS Jacob 5:52-54 | [2] **RLDS 2Nephi 12:42** / LDS 2Nephi 29:1 | [3] **RLDS Jacob 3:123-124** / LDS Jacob 5:60

47 And the Lord of the vineyard saith unto His servant: Go, therefore, send angels again to the land, and call servants, that we may labor diligently with all force in My vineyard, that we may prepare the way by which I may obtain again the natural fruit of the vineyard, a fruit that it will be good and more precious than any other fruit, and so let us work this last time, with all the commitment you need to rescue My vineyard, for the end is near; and it will be the last time that I will prune the trees of My vineyard[1]. [1] **RLDS Jacob 3:125-126** / LDS Jacob 5:61-62

48 And the branches shall be planted again; beginning with the last, that they may be the first, and that the former be the last; and dig around the trees, both old and new, the first and the last; and the last and the first, so that 'all come back' to be treated for the last time. So dig around them and prune them and fertilize them again, for the last time, because the end is near. And if these last grafts develop and produce the natural fruit, then I will prepare the way for them, so that they may grow and remain united in Me, the Lord of the vineyard[1]. [1] RLDS Jacob 3:127-129 / LDS Jacob 5:63-64

49 And as they begin to grow, you will take away the branches that bear fruit, that is, bitter feelings, according to the strength and size of the good; and you shall not take away the wicked all at once, lest the roots become too strong for the graft, and your graft die, and I lose the trees of My vineyard again; therefore, you will remove the evil feelings as the good ones grow, so that the root and the tree tops have the same strength, until the good feelings overpower the bad and the bad are cut and thrown into the fire; and so I will consume the wicked out of My vineyard forever[1]. [1] RLDS Jacob 3:130-132 / LDS Jacob 5:65-66

50 And the branches of the natural tree I will graft in the natural branches of the tree; and I will gather them again, that they may bring forth the natural fruit; and they shall be one in Me again, the Lord of the vineyard; for how much, the wicked shall be thrown out, even out of all the land of My vineyard; and burned, for behold, only this time will more I prune My vineyard[1]. [1] RLDS Jacob 3:133-135 / LDS Jacob 5:68-69

51 And it came to pass that the Lord of the vineyard sent His servant[1]; and the servant did as the Lord commanded him[2], and brought other servants; and were few[3]. [1] RLDS D&C 98:7d / LDS D&C 101:55 | [2] RLDS D&C 98:8c / LDS D&C 101:62 | [3] RLDS Jacob 3:136 / LDS Jacob 5:70

52 And the Lord of the vineyard said to them, Go and work in the vineyard with all your might, for behold, this is the last time that I have dealt with My vineyard; because the end is near and is rapidly approaching; and if you work busy with Me, then I will have joy in the fruit that I will keep for Myself, in the time that will soon come when these fruits will be essential to keep you united in the last days, that ye may work hard in My vineyard for the last time; and I, the Lord of the vineyard, will also work with you; if you obey My commandments in all things[1]. [1] RLDS Jacob 3:137-140 / LDS Jacob 5:71-72

53 And thus, the vineyard will return to produce the natural fruit; and the natural branches will begin to grow and develop greatly; and the wild branches will begin to be plucked and thrown away in order to preserve the equality of strength between the root and the tree canopy. And so these chosen servants will work with all diligence, according to the commandments of the Lord of the vineyard, until the wicked are thrown out of the vineyard, and the Lord has preserved for himself the righteous trees, the plantation of Jehovah[1].

[1] Isaiah 61:3

54 These, will become again in the natural fruit, whose roots will be firmly established next to the source of clean water[1]; and they have become as one body, whose fruits will be equal; and the Lord of the vineyard will preserve for himself the natural fruit of this tree, that is, the 'chosen seed' in relation to His vineyard in the last days, which will be very precious to Him from the beginning of the fullness of time[2]. [1] Jeremiah 17:8 | [2] RLDS Jacob 3:141-144 / LDS Jacob 5: 73-74

55 And it came to pass that when the Lord of the vineyard saw that his fruit was good, and that His vineyard was no more corrupt, He called His servants, and said unto them: Behold, for the last time we have tended My vineyard, and see that I have done according to My will; and I have kept the natural fruit, which is good, even as it was in the beginning. And blessed are ye because ye were diligent in working with Me in My vineyard for the last time, and because ye kept My commandments, and you brought again the natural fruit unto Me, the Lord.

56 Behold, My workers shall rejoice with Me because of the fruit of My vineyard in the last days. Behold, therefore, when the time cometh when bad fruit shall appear again in My vineyard, that I will separate the good fruit of bad fruit; the good fruit, I will keep for Myself, but the bad ones I will throw in their own place. And then comes the time and the end; and I will cause My vineyard to be burned with fire[1]. [1] RLDS Jacob 3:145-153 / LDS Jacob 5:75-77

57 And now, making use of some of the words of Jacob, verily, verily, I say unto you, The things that the prophet Zenos said concerning the house of Israel, comparing it to a good olive tree, surely shall come to pass. And on the day when I the Lord shall again stretch out My hand a second time to recover My people[1], it will be the day, yea, the last time that the servants of the Lord will, with their power, take care of His vineyard and will prune it; and after that, soon the end will come[2]. [1] RLDS 2Nephi 12:42 / LDS 2Nephi 29:1 | [2] RLDS Jacob 4:1-3 / LDS Jacob 6:1-2

58 Behold, will you reject these words preserved by My own hand for a wise future purpose? Will you reject the words of the prophets and all the words spoken by Me, Jesus Christ, in this record? Will you deny the power of God and the gift of the Holy Spirit[1] given to thee by the laying on of hands of those who have authority to do so[2]? [1] RLDS 2Nephi 12:31-39 / LDS 2Nephi 28:26-31 | [2] RLDS Jacob 4:12-13 /LDS Jacob 6:8

59 Behold, in so doing, you will erase forever the flame of the Holy Spirit who dwells in your heart, and with this attitude you will mock the grand plan of redemption that has been established for you since the foundation of the world. — Know ye not that if ye will do these things, that the power of the redemption and the resurrection, which is in Me, Jesus Christ, will bring you with shame and terrible guilt at the judgment seat of God on the last day[1]? [1] RLDS Jacob 4:14 / LDS Jacob 6:9

60 O, My beloved sons, repent ye and enter in at the strait gate, and continue in the way which is narrow, until ye shall obtain eternal life, until I shall meet you before the pleasing bar of God, which bar striketh the wicked with awful dread and fear. Amen[1]. [1] RLDS Jacob 4:16-18 / LDS Jacob 6:11-13

REFERENCE LIST

RLDS – versification used in scriptures published by the Reorganized Church of Jesus Christ of Latter Day Saints, Independence, Missouri.

LDS – versification used in scriptures published by The Church of Jesus Christ of Latter Day Saints, Salt Lake City, Utah.

IV – The Holy Scriptures, Translated and Corrected by the Spirit of Revelation by Joseph Smith Jr., the Seer.

RCH – The History of the Reorganized Church of Jesus Christ of Latter Day Saints, published by Herald House, Independence, Missouri.

Book of Tobit – (The book of Tobias) – apocryphal work found in the Roman Catholic canon via the Septuagint.

Made in the USA
Middletown, DE
22 November 2019